D1598114

Sensible Speculating

with

Put and Call Options

The limited-risk way to make money
in the stock market

by Sherwood Gaylord

Simon and Schuster / New York

Copyright © 1976 by Sherwood B. Gaylord
All rights reserved
including the right of reproduction
in whole or in part in any form
Published by Simon and Schuster
A Gulf+Western Company
Rockefeller Center, 630 Fifth Avenue
New York, New York 10020

Designed by Irving Perkins
Manufactured in the United States of America

1 2 3 4 5 6 7 8 9 10

Library of Congress Cataloging in Publication Data

Gaylord, Sherwood B.
    Sensible speculating with put and call options.

    Includes index.
    1.   Put and call transactions.   I.   Title.
HG6041.G39   332.6'45   76-16547
ISBN 0-671-22322-4

To Lois, my wife, who could hardly care less about options, but nevertheless scattered question marks throughout eight drafts, persisting until the text was understandable to her and presumably would be clear even to other readers with no option experience and only superficial knowledge of the stock market.

Contents

Foreword ═══════════════════

Sherwood Gaylord was born with a natural ability to clarify difficult subjects for readers of technical material. He has now coupled this talent with a long-time interest in finance, stocks and options.

In my opinion, his book is a clear presentation of sensible ways to participate in the option markets, whether on an ultra-conservative, highly speculative or in-between basis. It gives clear explanations of twenty different ways to use options, provides the first list of optionable stocks arranged by industry, offers simple rules of thumb for evaluating premiums, and presents many other original ideas.

Appropriate metaphors make the fundamentals easy to understand and are often good for a chuckle. All in all, this is a book that can be read easily by anyone who has a modicum of experience with common stocks.

Other good option books are available, but Mr. Gaylord's is surely the most fun to read and presently the most up-to-date—an interesting and valuable source of information and ideas for all who have a desire to gain a better understanding of how they may use listed puts and calls safely and profitably.

> JAMES W. CARPENTER
> Manager, Option Department
> Spencer Trask & Co. Incorporated

Introduction ════════════════

Within the lifetime of most adults, air has become man's third media for public transportation. Previously, for thousands of years, travel was limited to the slow pace and hazards of moving directly over land and water, but today millions fly to their goals safely—ten times faster than ever before.

In the investment world, marketable options are an even newer third medium, supplementing bonds and stocks just as the air has added a new dimension to land and water travel. In a similar way these new options can take you safely to investment goals ten times faster than the older media—when controlled by a knowledgeable operator.

Of course, not every traveler likes to fly, or needs to; nor are options for every investor. However, since options are already influencing these older forms of investments, lack of knowledge about options may become a costly void in your investment skills, even though you do not now plan to enter this market. Why?

· Your broker and investor friends undoubtedly refer to options in relation to stocks. To understand their comments and be able to communicate with them, some knowledge of the basic role of modern options in investment portfolio management is essential.

· Heavy option activity may occasionally affect the price of an underlying stock in your portfolio. Wouldn't you like to understand why?

· Any decision not to participate in option trading, based on your indifference or lack of knowledge, may have been made too hastily. Among four basic option strategies, which cover a broad spectrum of more than 20 different profitable techniques, surely some would help you at least occasionally to meet personal investment objectives more effectively.

Of 25,000,000 shareowners in the United States, probably less than 1 percent could be considered option experts now, although the number is growing rapidly. So if you don't understand options—how and why they can be profitable—no need to feel embarrassed; you have lots of company!

Most investors who presently do understand options have acquired their knowledge through close association with an experienced broker, or through costly personal trial-and-error trading experiences. Very little information is available to lead inexperienced potential option traders through a wide variety of strategies designed to fulfill personal investment goals.

It is important to understand at the start that option trading should not lead you to a different set of investment goals than you have previously determined are best for your individual situation. Rather, it should help you to achieve these existing goals. For example:

> · If you are interested in receiving greater income from your stocks than current dividends yield, options can provide it.
> · If you are interested in a more rapid increase in capital gains, options can give them to you with jetlike speed. (Of course, these two goals require two different option strategies.)
> · If your need is to own stocks in a manner which provides substantial assurance against immediate capital loss, options offer a method to obtain that protection.

There are many other benefits enjoyed by option traders but for starters it would seem that at least one of these should meet at least one need of most investors.

If this all sounds like a scheme whereby you can have your cake and eat it too—it isn't. With options, as in most other business transactions, to receive one benefit you must give up another. In other words, you make a trade-off, receiving something you want or need now in exchange for something else that is of less value to you at the present time.

Favorable option trade-offs are generally available to you because not many investors have identical strategies. The basic approach is to decide what it is you want more of—for example, income, growth, protection or tax advantages—then determine whether or not these benefits are worth whatever it is you must give up to obtain them.

The reason there is such a great sudden interest in CBOE (Chicago Board Options Exchange), AMEX (American Stock Exchange), PHLX (Philadelphia Exchange) and PSE (Pacific Stock Exchange) options today is that these marketable options were only invented in 1973. Before then it would not have been possible for you to make these option trade-offs at any price.

We will be examining these option benefits in detail throughout the book, so perhaps we should now take a brief look at the nature of this new form of security.

To help understand the nature of options we might use an analogy between the rental of an automobile and purchase of a call option. For example, there are more than 100 leading common stocks that you may rent for periods of a few days to nearly nine months, much as you would rent a car from Hertz or Avis. When you buy a call option, in effect, you sign a lease which gives you the use of its underlying stock (less dividends) for the life of the option, or until you choose to terminate the agreement.

Why should anyone want to rent a stock? Of the four basic reasons, three are the same ones which might prompt you to rent from Hertz, instead of buying a car.

· A rental requires less cash or debt than does an outright purchase.
· Total maximum cost of each trip can be determined in advance.
· When you no longer need or desire to continue its use, the agreement and expense can be terminated easily.

The fourth reason for renting vis-à-vis owning a stock is different. You would rent a stock only when you expected to make a profit on it during the rental period. If you believe that the stock will decline in value while you own the option, you obviously would not be interested in either renting or owning it.

You may have noticed that option language uses several common words which have been given special meanings. An understanding of just seven terms is all you need right now. These are defined briefly by CBOE (Chicago Board Options Exchange) as follows:

OPTION: A contract allowing the buyer to buy or sell 100 shares of stock at a specific price during a specific period of time, regardless of the market price of that stock.

CALL: An option contract giving the buyer a right to purchase the stock.

PUT: An option contract giving the buyer a right to sell the stock.

EXPIRATION DATE: The date on which an option contract expires; the last day on which an option can be exercised.

EXERCISE (OR STRIKING) PRICE: The price at which the buyer of a call can purchase the stock during the life of the option, or the buyer of a put can sell the stock.

PREMIUM: The price the buyer pays the writer for an option contract. The term "premium" is synonymous with the "price" of a marketable option.

WRITER: The grantor of an option contract. Also called the "maker."

The words "call" and "option" were often used interchangeably prior to the introduction of marketable puts. Either type of option is merely a legal agreement between two investors (through their brokers and an option exchange) whereby one party agrees to sell (or buy in the case of a put) 100 shares of a specific stock at any time prior to the stated option expiration—if the buyer decides to buy it (or sell if a put). This agreement actually is a form of security, traded on the major option exchanges every business day, just as the common stock which it represents is traded on the New York Stock Exchange.

The reason this little contract between you and an unidentified second party can be traded on a national exchange, just like other marketable securities, is that there are thousands of investors all over the country who are also interested in buying and selling identical calls. The exchange stores all of these identical contracts in a computer so you never know or care from whom you bought your call or to whom you might have sold it.

Authorized floor traders are present on the exchanges at all times to maintain a continuous market. They are willing to sell the options of that exchange to you when no public sellers are interested, and to buy when you want to sell and no outside buyers can be found. In other words, it is always possible to execute a market order to buy or sell an option during normal exchange hours. This instant liquidity or marketability of options is the spectacular innovation created by CBOE in 1973.

The reason options can be exchange-traded now, rather than negotiated individually over the counter, is that only relatively few kinds of standardized calls are ever created. These exchange-traded options are limited to:

· Only a relatively few stocks, now less than 200, on CBOE, AMEX, PHLX and PSE. When related to their options, stocks are referred to as the "underlying stock."

· Four standardized expiration dates per year on any one stock. The actual life of identical options will vary, depending on when each was purchased. However, option life is never more than nine months. All identical options expire automatically at the same instant, except for those which have been previously terminated.

· One or more specific striking prices—the price at which 100 shares of the stock can be purchased by the option buyer. When an option is created the striking price is always near the current market value of the underlying stock and is divisible by five. Later a choice of several striking prices may be available if the market value of the stock recently has fluctuated over a wide price range.

"Premium" is simply the price paid for the option. It is usually expressed in dollars and fractions of a dollar per share. For example, an option which sold for 2½ would cost $250 ($2.50 per share times 100) plus the commission.

"Writer" is merely another name for the original seller of the option: the person ready at all times to deliver 100 shares of the stock at the striking price, when demanded to do so by the holder of the call. The seller must deliver the 100 shares of stock to the buyer *at the buyer's option,* even though otherwise he could sell it at a higher price on the open market. To offset this disadvantage, the seller receives a fairly substantial payment, called the premium, when he sells the call. This extra income has a very beneficial effect in reducing potential risk and increasing the yield of his investment portfolio.

Opportunities to use options in so many kinds of situations makes them fascinating and rewarding for most investors who understand their applications.

Options may seem complicated at first, but they are not really difficult to understand after a little bit of study. To help simplify the subject for you, this book is divided into seven parts. Part I explains basic mechanics of options in everyday language. Part II then covers a type of option application easiest to understand—the simple purchase of a call. Part III discusses several conservative ways to increase investment profit and protect your stock by selling calls, rather than by buying them. Part IV takes you through a wide variety of methods for investment hedging by the use of options. Part V outlines the most bearish approach—selling unprotected or naked calls. Part VI applies some information you will have acquired about calls to the newer field of puts. Part VII, finally, looks to the future of options.

Investors use a wide range of strategies all the way from ultraconservative to highly speculative. Some advance in their skills and interest to the simultaneous buying and selling of combinations of similar options and consider this a sophisticated form of entertainment. Certainly Parker Brothers has never produced a game with more adult challenge and excitement. So, whatever your approach, welcome to the ever-growing group of participants in this great new world of options. "Investigate before you invest" and give all your calls the ring of success!

PART I

Understanding Options

1

Why Call at All?

What reason would you possibly have for buying an option? True, their popularity has grown at a faster rate than any new form of negotiable security in modern times—yet they pay no dividends or interest; commissions are a high percentage of total cost, and they may expire worthless in only a few months if not actively supervised.

Then look at the attractive competitive investments which are bidding for the money that might go into options. Savings accounts and bonds pay the highest interest in decades. Gifts ranging from alarm clocks to color TV sets often are given free when you open an account. Many quality common stocks are earning (but not paying) 20% or more on their present market value instead of the usual 5 or 10%. Yet option trading is growing by leaps and bounds.

There are just two basic reasons for the immense popularity of options. Number one is *inflation*. Personal experience tells all of us that the money we have saved really earns nothing; in fact, it erodes when inflation increases faster than the rate of total income it produces.

Double-digit inflation has left not only a poignant memory of the recent past, but a deep concern that it will return in the near future. That is why many are groping to find an investment medium that will give them a total return of interest, dividends or capital appreciation greater than the expected inflation rate. Otherwise, when their investment and its accumulated income is turned back into dollars, it will buy fewer goods and services than it would have, even before the investment was made.

19

Option traders recognize that the most conservative option approach—selling calls against stock they own—should yield a minimum of 20% annually. With a more speculative option strategy, the sky is the limit, although such a program does involve greater risk. The point of this, of course, is that even the most conservative option program can yield more than the highest known rate of inflation, protecting the future purchasing power of an investment, and leaving something additional for the use of an investor's money.

The second reason for the popularity of options is the burning desire of many persons to obtain better-than-average performance from their investments. Extensive studies have been made by universities, large brokerage firms and other institutions about the average long-term yield of a portfolio of common stocks. These studies all demonstrate that a selection of diversified stocks, held continuously for several decades, has had a total return (dividends and appreciation) of from about 7 to 9%. In the absence of high inflation, this return would be fairly attractive. Today, however, such a low return is inadequate—it provides no real income.

Many investors are disturbed by another group of study conclusions. These indicate that a portfolio made up of stocks selected by throwing darts at the stock transaction page of *The Wall Street Journal* would, over an extended period of time, have performed just as well as a scientific selection made with all the advanced financial analytical techniques available. This conclusion may not always be true, but many experts believe that over a long period it is generally correct. This is called the "Random Walk" theory.

No wonder many option enthusiasts are among those who have examined these two seemingly unsolvable problems, and have determined not to stand by passively and see the purchasing power of their savings erode. Most of them understand that successful option trading will demand that they take time to understand the nature of options and the different ways of using them. No broker or financial service can do all your thinking and planning for you in a way that best meets your personal financial position and priorities.

If you decide to trade options on more than an occasional hit-

or-miss basis, you should prepare to spend relatively more time supervising your option portfolio than you would for an equal investment in stocks and bonds.

The amazing growth of option trading is based on a desire by many investors to avoid erosion of their savings and thereby obtain a respectable return from a more inflation-proof form of investment. For most of us it has required much effort and self-discipline to accumulate our savings. Therefore, isn't it wise to devote a little more effort and self-discipline to preserving and making these funds grow? One way is to acquire the knowledge necessary to make effective use of options.

Of course, you can start to trade options immediately. No one is going to test your competence before you begin. You don't even have to show your broker a license to rent his stocks, as you would be required to show Hertz a driver's license before they would permit you to rent their car.

A broker's experience in options can help you—in fact, this is a necessity. But brokers are in a much better position to assist with suggestions when you already have an in-depth understanding of the things they may discuss, so that you can make your own decisions.

You could rent a car to go somewhere, in a geographical sense. You can also rent a stock to go somewhere, but in your chosen financial direction. With either vehicle, it pays to know your present situation and where you want the rental to take you. Skill in following the rules of the road is essential in either case.

Options are less well understood than automobiles—not because they are more complicated, but simply because they are so new, and relatively few persons have had an opportunity to acquire experience in using them. Today we almost assume that a person is born with competence to operate a car. But my grandfather, a retired farmer, understood options (on real estate) much better than automobiles. He bought a Brisco in 1920, but he only drove it once—two blocks from the dealer's garage through the end of his own carriage shed!

Likewise, investors who have heard about options can move ahead without preparation, as grandfather did when he switched from a horse to a car. Fortunately he wasn't hurt, but inexperienced option traders may not be so lucky. They are traveling bumper to bumper on a fast national thoroughfare, competing against huge financial institutions and professionals.

Except for some brief superficial magazine articles, a few rather technical books, and limited broker-sponsored option-sales meetings, at present there is no facility or definitive source of information generally available for the public to acquire option expertise that would be similar to skills taught in a driving school.

During the ten years prior to the introduction of marketable options by CBOE in 1973, I was an active trader in over-the-counter options. This was the best option "school" available to investors, but there were relatively few students compared with the numbers of persons now interested in the subject. These new options are attracting millions who have no previous option experience. Will they suffer a fate similar to that of grandfather with his Brisco—or worse?

What could protect them? Literally hundreds of seemingly redundant books are published about the stock market in general, but very few on options.

No one can guarantee profits or give assurance that you will have no losses. However, a good book can help you to understand the basic nature of options, the relationship between risk and reward in twenty or more different option routes, and guide you toward those strategies most likely to be compatible with your nature and investment situation.

This book aims to provide just such help for the novice and experienced option trader alike. For this reason Part I uses a few homey analogies and simple option examples to let you test the water before suggesting that you plunge in over your head.

So let's start out by asking, "Where in the world would you like to call?"

2

Where in the World Would You Like to Call?

It is commonly believed that options are nothing but an outright speculation—you either win big or lose all. This is not true. If it were, options might only be legal in Nevada.

To understand the variety of directions in the investment world where calls can take you, visualize an option "map" with North as "Up" and South as "Down." Specifically, use North for "added income with lower risk," and South for "added leverage with higher risk." Then East will represent "added protection," and West "tax advantages." When we place these points on a compass they might look like Figure 1.

In this chapter we begin to examine ways of using calls for travel in each of these four investment directions, plus certain combinations of them.

Greater Income—This is a very simple low-risk way to use options. Many persons believe it is also the most rewarding. To go this way, you first select an optionable stock already in your portfolio or buy one you would like to own. Then instruct your broker to sell a specific call option. He will sell the call "short" and hold your stock certificate so as to be prepared to make delivery of stock in case the buyer chooses to exercise the call.

You will decide which expiration month to write and the striking price at which your stock can be purchased, should the buyer exercise the call. Your decisions will be influenced by the relationships of prices then offered, for various option lives and striking prices. Detailed suggestions to help make such decisions are presented in Part III.

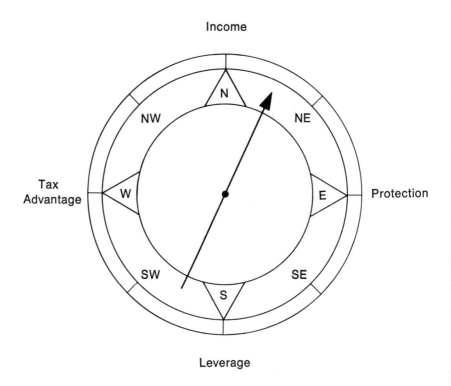

Figure 1. *An option compass for pointing your calls in the direction of your established investment goals.*

Having made these decisions and sold a call, the action will unfold in about this sequence:

· You immediately receive a check or credit for several hundred dollars from your broker. This represents the option premium (price), less a commission of about $25. A six-month call should give you about 10% of the market value of the stock. Then, if your six-month plan is repeated twice each year, two 10% premiums, plus dividends on the stock, should provide about a 25% annual rate of return.

· Next, you merely wait and let the market do your work for you. Generally the most favorable situation you should hope for is an advance in the stock price.

· If this occurs rapidly you might wish to buy back the option and rewrite another at a higher striking price. In this case you would have an advantageous tax situation and the option would have pointed you in a northwesterly direction.

· As the option nears its expiration date and the stock price is above the striking price you will need to decide whether or not to repurchase the option. If you wish to keep the stock, you should repurchase. If not, the call will be exercised and your stock sold. There are tax advantages either way, as will be explained in later chapters.

· The option will expire worthless if, at the end of its life, the stock is selling below the striking price. Then all of the premium will be yours to keep as additional income. This situation moves you in a direction which is a combination of greater income and protection of capital. Our option compass would point in a northeasterly direction.

Greater Protection of Capital—Options can protect your capital in two quite different situations:

· You already own the stock, or
· You don't own it now but would like to buy if you could be guaranteed that its price would not fall more than a few percent during the next six months.

If you own a stock and are concerned that its price might drop during the next few months, you could sell a call, just as described above under "Greater Income." Then if the price of the stock did decline your option premium would offset about 10% of the drop, depending on the call sold. Refer again to our compass and you will note that this would correspond to calling in a northeasterly direction.

To illustrate the second type of protection, assume that you wish to acquire a stock which you do not now own, provided you could limit risk of an immediate sharp decline. In this case you would buy (not sell) a call on the stock. This would assure you of the right to purchase the stock at the striking price during the entire life of your call, no matter how high the stock price might rise during that time. An even more important protection for the option buyer, however, may be limitation of loss, should the stock price fall sharply. If this happens the call could be resold and part of the premium salvaged. Even if the call were left to expire worthless, however, your maximum loss would be no more than the premium—perhaps 10% of the stock price. In situations where the stock price falls sharply, purchase of a stock rather than its call nearly always creates a larger dollar loss.

To see how purchase of a call affords outstanding protection to a prospective buyer of its underlying stock, consider the example of Avon Products during the 1973–74 period. When the stock was selling in the range of from $100 to $140 per share, a three- to six-month call would have cost about 10% of the market price of the stock, or $10 to $14 a share.

Such a call probably would not have been profitable under any circumstance. However, even if it were held until it became worthless, the total loss would have been only $10 to $14 per share. Compare this with perhaps a $100 per share loss, suffered by those investors who owned or purchased the stock at around $140, and stayed with it all the way down to $19 a share. A call would have avoided most of this great dollar loss, without diminishing the opportunity for gain (less the cost of the call), had the price of Avon advanced, as most of its owners must have expected it to do.

Greater Leverage—The price of a call may range from 1 or 2% of the stock's market price, for very short-term calls, to between 10 and 20% for options with a life of six to eight months. A typical six-months' call will have a premium equal to about 10% of the stock's market price.

When the stock price and the striking price are nearly identical, the call premium will advance about $100 for each one dollar per share increase in the stock price. To illustrate this leverage, assume you have purchased an option on a $50 stock for a $500 premium. This represents a call on $5000 worth of stock. When the stock price advances one point or $100 per 100 shares, the call will advance by nearly the same amount. For simplicity, let's assume that it does.

The $500 invested in a call will then increase to $600, while 100 shares of the underlying stock advances by $100 to $5,100. The percentage increases are: option value 20%, the stock only 2%. In other words, the option increased 10 times faster. The leverage of the option vis-à-vis the stock was, therefore, 10 to 1.

Unfavorable leverage for the call occurs when the stock price declines. This is an ever-present possibility, which should be understood before any call is purchased. However, if you are determined to maintain a position in a stock while its price is in a declining trend, even a call that expires worthless may subject you to far lower dollar loss than you would have experienced had the underlying stock been purchased and held instead.

Options can provide very dramatic leverage up and down. Consider, for example, this IBM illustration.

During a single week in January 1975 IBM common stock rose $25 per share, or about 15%. In that same week IBM April 160 calls rose 118% and the April 220 calls were up 268%. Let's assume that you had been interested in buying IBM stock the previous Friday. For $16,300 you could have purchased 100 shares of the stock. To put an equal amount into IBM calls would have been sheer folly even to consider as an alternative but, for the purpose of illustrating leverage, let's assume that you did.

That sum of money would have, theoretically at least, purchased 11 April 160 calls or 163 April 220's. One week later the score on these three alternative investments would have been about as follows:

An Investment of $16,300 in:	Increased to	For a $ Increase of	Or a % Gain of
100 Shares IBM	$18,825	$ 2,537	15%
11 April 160 Calls	35,200	18,900	118
163 April 220 Calls	59,820	43,520	268

This example is given merely to show the very powerful leverage of calls compared with their underlying stock. In April, when IBM stock was below $220 per share, those calls expired worthless. In other words, the $16,300 which had grown to $59,820 in one week fell to zero within three months. Leverage works both ways!

When the number of calls purchased corresponds to the number of round lots (100 shares) of the stock you otherwise would have bought, your investment direction is a combination of protection and greater leverage—southeasterly on our compass.

If, however, you were to buy far more calls than the number of round lots of underlying stock you would or could have purchased, your compass needle would swing due south.

There is nothing wrong in pointing your option compass in any direction you please, as long as you know where you are headed, and that the direction chosen is compatible with your personal situation.

Greater Tax Advantages—Whether you choose to head in the direction of greater income or of more leverage, any tax advantage you can pick up along the way should be quite welcome. Marketable options have opened potential tax shelters.

If you are new to options, these tax shelters may not seem so simple now. However, as you progress through subsequent chapters, you will find that they are relatively easy to understand and use. They have some definite benefits over older shelters, such as limited oil-royalty partnerships and cattle raising.

Here are two examples:

· If you head toward greater income via option writing, the premium income automatically becomes a long-term capital gain, if the stock is called and it has been held over six months.

· If the option price increases, due to an advance in the price of its underlying stock, you might decide to buy back the call at a "loss," since it is fully deductible. The attractive feature of this situation is that there is certain to be a simultaneous and larger offsetting increase in the value of your underlying stock. This can be a future long-term capital gain.

Our option-compass analogy is not quite a perfect fit for this example because you can be heading east (protection) and west (tax advantage) as well as north (income)—all at the same time! It's almost like having your cake and eating it too, but not quite, as we shall see in later chapters.

Briefly, it is like this: If you repurchased an option at exactly the same price you sold it for originally, there would be, of course, no income-tax deduction. You have received a needed "bear market insurance" protection at no real cost.*

No option route is perfectly smooth or certain to take you to your investment goals merely because you point the compass in a specific direction. Obstacles can pop up along the way that require expert navigational skills. Favorable timing is extremely important. Even before you start your journey there are three factors you should check out.

· Is your proposed option plan in accord with your current personal investment philosophy? Do you understand the possible risks and are you prepared to change course if the climate becomes too unfavorable?

· Is the overall stock market trend moving in a direction compatible with your option plan?

· Are the specific underlying stock and its options in a trend favorable for your approach? If you are selling, is the premium high enough? If buying, is the premium low enough?

Of necessity, this chapter presents an oversimplified and superficial explanation of option trading. This has been done to make a basic point: that options can take you to nearly any point on an investment compass—a valuable concept of option versatility with which many investors seem not to be familiar.

Any decision regarding suitable directions for you to take in future option trading should be deferred a little longer until your knowledge of this new option vehicle is more firmly established. Then, too, before you select a specific route and a favorable time,

---

* Unexercised call premiums were originally thought to be taxable as ordinary income, if profitable—a reduction in ordinary income if repurchased at a loss. The Mikva bill made all unexercised option premiums short-term capital gains or losses and thereby removed any possibility of gains or losses in ordinary income through option writing. The highly publicized option income "tax shelters" previously available are no longer valid.

it should be useful to acquire a more thorough understanding of the advantages and risks of various alternatives.

So, let's increase our understanding of the option vehicle by looking under the hood. Then we can disassemble and study the various components of the option machine to see what makes it tick.

3

Lift the Hood—and the Mystery

"Investigate before you invest" applies to options even more than to stocks. But first we need to investigate what it is about options that needs investigation. In other words, what goes on under the hood of the option vehicle that enables it to take off in so many attractive directions at such a low cost?

We know the four basic parts used: *underlying stock, striking price, expiration month,* and *premium.* Now we need to understand what there is about this assembly of parts that can take us safely in our chosen investment direction.

An automotive vehicle moves us because latent energy in gasoline is converted into mechanical power; likewise, an option functions because its engine converts time into money. In options, time is synonymous with remaining life. We will, therefore, lump these two terms together as we try to understand how the option mechanism performs this conversion necessary to propel every option vehicle.

Time and Life—Equating time with money is not new. Banks pay interest on time deposits, tenants buy occupancy time with rent money. These rather mundane examples of "Time is money" are illustrations of its value in a rigid form, and about as exciting as a block of marble.

Options, however, resemble time which is similar to marble after it has been placed in the hands of sculptors. Infinite designs can be created in either medium. Another similarity is that the resulting value of the product, in either case, may vary over a wide range because its worth depends on changing opinions and tastes of the public markets as well as on the designer's skill. Options, like sculpture, are more exciting to possess than stocks or blocks of marble, but in return each exposes its owner to greater risk.

While this comparison between options and sculpture may illustrate the great flexibility available to creators in either field, in another respect it calls attention to the characteristic in which options and sculpture are poles apart—permanence.

Marble is forever; but an option has a predetermined death date the instant it is created. This is subject to change only if it is executed sooner. Because of this predetermined end of life, options are classified as "wasting assets." Their value automatically declines a little each day unless some outside force pushes it up. For a call, such basic external force could only be an increase in the market value of its underlying stock.

As an efficiency-minded person, you may react by thinking that you certainly would not want to own a wasting asset. Don't be too sure. After all, every elective office is another form of wasting asset, including that of the President of the United States. Look how coveted these wasting assets are!

The previous chapter was designed to start you thinking of possible answers to the question, "In what directions should I plan to go?" As we try to discover in this chapter what it is that makes the option engine run, we also begin to face the second question: "What is a fair price for going this way?" Nearly every page in this book is designed to help you answer these two key questions more successfully.

An important prerequisite to successful option trading is the ability to evaluate instantly and automatically the worth to you of any option's time value. Other investors and floor traders or specialists on the option exchanges are making their evaluations constantly.

When a buyer and seller are in agreement on a price, it doesn't necessarily mean that either is mistaken in regard to the option's time value. Each has a different set of needs or reasons for buying or selling—his compass may be pointed in a different direction from yours. So, when the time value of a specific option is worth more to you than it is to willing sellers, you are presented with a profitable buying opportunity; if the situation is reversed, an opportunity to sell.

The option premium is the time value when the stock is selling below the striking price. Time value is less than the premium for calls which are in the money—in other words, when the stock is selling for more than the striking price. For all in-the-money calls, the time value is equal to premium minus the intrinsic value. To understand this, of course, we must first see what intrinsic value is all about.

Intrinsic Value—The intrinsic value of a call is always exactly equal to the current price of the underlying stock minus the call's striking price. It is the exercise value the call has at that instant.

To test your understanding, what would be the intrinsic value of a $40 call on General Electric with an $8 premium when the stock was trading at $45? Answer: The stock price, $45, minus the striking price, $40, equals $5, the intrinsic value of a call on one share. The exercise or intrinsic value of a call on 100 shares would be the current price of 100 GE shares ($4,500), less the striking price of 100 shares ($4,000), or $500. The remaining $300 of premium is the call's time value.

Whenever you examine an in-the-money call premium, it is good practice to think of intrinsic value and time value separately. You can assume that you will nearly always pay or receive 100 cents for every dollar of intrinsic value. However, the market price of time value is flexible, and it is on this factor that your subjective analysis will differ from that of others, thereby occasionally creating very attractive option exchange opportunities.

The Worth of Time Value to You—Because of your own personal goals, you probably place a different worth on time value when you are a prospective seller of a specific option than you would if you were a prospective buyer at that same instant.

Assume, for example, that you are the prospective buyer of a certain company's stock. How much would it be worth to you, through purchase of a call, to receive the benefits for which you are looking, yet be able to continue using most of the purchase cost (represented by the striking price) for other purposes during the life of the call? At prevailing rates of interest and inflation,

12% per year, or 1% per month, would seem a reasonable minimum.

But when buying a call, you expect to pay an additional premium for the "insurance" value, protecting you against any substantial drop in value you might experience if you owned stock instead of the call. Were your position reversed, and you took this risk as the seller of a call, you would certainly want to receive some premium, perhaps at least an additional 1% per month.

There are a number of other considerations you should evaluate in setting a price on time value. One of these is a measure of the stock's price volatility, known as its Beta factor. This subject will be presented later. For simplicity now, we can merely add the 1% capital charge to a 1% risk factor. So somewhere in the area of a 2% per month charge for time value has been a sort of watershed figure, separating the more attractive areas for buying and for selling. We must remember, of course, that the total premium consists of time value plus any intrinsic value.

This 2% rough "rule of thumb" for time value applies only to calls which have a striking price nearly identical with the stock price. Out-of-the-money calls, those with a striking price above the stock's price, have zero intrinsic value. The entire premium represents only time value, and this decreases at a very rapid rate as the stock drops farther away from the striking price. For example, with its stock at $60, the premium for a six-month $60 call on Xerox was about 1½% per month but on the same day a similar $70 call, $10 out of the money, sold for about ¾ of 1%, while the $80 call traded at ⅓ of 1% per month.

When calls are deep in the money their time value actually declines as the stock's price and option's intrinsic value increase. To illustrate, consider two or more calls identical except for striking prices, each with the same reasonable amount of remaining life. Their intrinsic values differ by exactly the same amount as the spread between the striking prices. You might expect that their premiums also would differ by exactly this same amount. Not so. For example, on a day when Polaroid closed at $36, the six-month $35 call was $7. Its intrinsic value was $1, so its time value was $6, or approximately 2% per month of remaining life. A similar $30 call sold for $10. Its intrinsic value was $6 so its time value was only $4, or just slightly over 1% per month.

You will nearly always find that with two similar in-the-money calls, the one with a lower striking price also will have a lower time value. The reason is logical. The higher intrinsic value of the premium requires a buyer to invest more money in that call. This increases his capital cost and risk. The seller thereby is relieved of a portion of the cost and risk and so is willing to accept a premium which reflects a lower amount for the option's time value.

When a new series of options is first offered for trading, with a remaining life of nearly nine months, or 180 days, one less day is not very significant. However, with only 15 or 20 days of life remaining, time value decays rapidly with the passing of each trading day. During the last week or two of life, most calls trade at or very near their intrinsic value, and with almost a zero time value.

It is quite obvious at this point that when you purchase a call you are buying time. But, time for what? Actually, it is to wait for something to change the price of a certain common stock. In the final analysis, an option's value is totally dependent on price changes in its underlying stock. That is why option profit opportunities are greatly influenced by the choice of underlying stocks—so let's look at them next.

Stocks with Exchange-Traded Options—To have its options traded on an exchange, a stock must meet several criteria. First, it is selected by an exchange as one whose options will be attractive to traders. This means that the corporation must be well known and popular, and that its stock has been actively traded.

The Securities and Exchange Commission must also approve all listings based on its criteria. For example, the corporation's dividends must not have exceeded earnings in any one of the last five years—a rule that prevented option trading in General Motors during CBOE's first two years.

A stock with exchange-traded options, therefore, has passed through a selection process more rigorous than was required for it to trade on the New York Stock Exchange.

Generally speaking, stocks with exchange-traded options are

the larger, more active NYSE institutional favorites that have been relatively consistent in their earnings growth and dividend-payment record. This should not imply, however, that these stocks have had higher dividends or earnings or that their stock price will perform any better than many other stocks which do not have listed options.

A current list of these stocks, and their option premiums, is now available in every issue of *The Wall Street Journal, Barron's, The New York Times,* and other periodicals.

Nearly all published tabulations of options are arranged by exchange and series, then alphabetically for easy pricing reference. When you are searching through these lists for a suitable option to buy or sell, you can very easily select one and overlook others in the same industry that may be even more attractive.

Although any option tabulation published in book form is certain to become obsolete, Appendix A does list by industry those corporations which had exchange-traded options at the time of publication.

Perhaps an option service will recognize a need for this kind of arrangement and publish up-to-date option data by industry. In any event, the purpose of this section of the Appendix is merely to remind you to look briefly at all the option opportunities for companies within an industry of your choice whenever you consider trading the options of any one company in that group.

Stocks with No Exchange-Traded Options—Stocks for which exchange-traded calls are not now available include many fine and popular corporations. However, both calls and puts can be purchased on nearly any publicly traded corporate stock, including AMEX issues or those traded over-the-counter. These options are the old "unique" OTC type previously mentioned, not traded on any option exchange and not readily resalable.

Because there is little or no resale market for this type of option, it is nearly impossible to capture any *time value.* Even part of the *intrinsic value* can be lost unless you exercise the option. You may be able to resell it to the dealer from whom it was purchased, but only on the basis of the intrinsic value, less two commissions on the stock.

There are two reasons why you might occasionally wish to trade in over-the-counter options despite these problems.

- You especially want options on a stock which has no exchange-traded options.
- You intend to hold the options until near their expiration date, or exercise them.

The Option Factories—Having lifted the hood and inspected the option mechanism, we can now move on to examine the option factories. Perhaps we should think of them as rental agencies for stocks. Either way, familiarity with option exchanges and the organizations that operate them should help us become more effective when we begin to trade.

CBOE, the Hertz of the option world, is Number One. In fact, from 1973 to 1975, CBOE was the only one. AMEX, although it did not start trading in options until 1975, is now in second place. PHLX, the Philadelphia Exchange, is a recent entry and a very distant third, and PSE, the Pacific Stock Exchange, is number four. Others plan to follow. So, let's look at the option exchanges, see what they do that can help you make money, and how they are equipped to do it.

4

CBOE Is the Hertz of Stock Rental—AMEX Is Avis

The Chicago Board Options Exchange (CBOE) deserves much credit for its innovative concepts, developed during several years of study prior to the 1973 debut of CBOE as the world's first stock-option auction market. Public acceptance was so rapid and enthusiastic that every major stock exchange except the Big Board (NYSE) quickly announced plans to follow the lead of CBOE and create a similar exchange.

The American Stock Exchange (AMEX) started trading options two years later, followed by the Philadelphia Exchange (PHLX). CBOE in stock rentals is clearly Number One, like Hertz in the car-rental field, while AMEX, the Avis of options, has been moving up fast in the Number Two spot.

As we view the spectacular success of option exchanges, so recently started from scratch, it is logical to wonder why option exchanges did not exist previously. Then as we begin to compare the pre-1973 over-the-counter (OTC) options with the amazing innovations incorporated into the new exchange-traded variety, we might modify our query to "How did CBOE manage to develop such an unusual system?"

Pre-Exchange Options—Stock options (puts and calls) are not new. They have been popular since the seventeenth century in England, where they were known as *privileges*. In the United States these OTC options were first called *papers* when they became popular in the nineteenth century. They had weaknesses similar to other contracts of that time—that is, their validity was only equal to the integrity and resources of the seller who signed them. There was a lack of dependability about these early options that continued into the early twentieth century. Option sellers frequently would disown their contracts, and this reneging caused many potential buyers to lose interest.

Seller reliability took a great leap forward shortly after passage of the Securities Act of 1933. A group of about 50 New York City dealers in options then joined to form the Put and Call Brokers and Dealers Association, Inc. It was in no sense an option exchange, but a self-regulating body of responsible dealers who recognized that if options were to survive they had to meet the urgent need for greater integrity in the industry.

Probably the Association's greatest contribution was an arrangement to sell options almost exclusively through NYSE member firms. These large brokerage houses endorsed each option they sold, thereby protecting buyers with a valid guarantee of performance.

This OTC options system is still functioning. It works something like this: Tell your NYSE broker of your interest in buying a call on a certain company's stock. His New York office will contact several put-and-call dealers for an indication of interest and competitive prices. These dealers in turn will call prospective option writers (sellers) whom they know, or check with other brokers to locate persons who might be interested in selling options to you. Finally, if this effort succeeds, the diverse interests of five or six individuals, institutions, and brokers will have been coordinated and an option agreement negotiated.

Although the Association and a few of its dealer firms continue in business, many former put-and-call dealers have closed. Exchange-traded options have so many advantages over old-style OTC varieties that these dealers cannot possibly compete.

It would be unfortunate if in the future none of these old-time dealers remain in the OTC option business. They are still needed because even today exchange options are listed on less than 10% of all NYSE stocks, only one AMEX issue (Syntex) and no OTC stocks. An investor interested in buying an option on any company which has no option on an exchange probably can still find a broker to arrange for an OTC option, through one of these few remaining New York put-and-call dealers.

So, there has been an option market in the United States for over a century—but it provided only for the original purchase and sale. Prior to CBOE, the missing ingredient was an auction floor where existing options could be exchanged easily, at a resale price that permitted the owner-reseller to capture the option's *time value.*

Most OTC calls are created with the stock price and option striking price identical. This means that intrinsic value is zero. The premium is substantial, usually 2% per month or more of the stock price, but it all goes into *time value.* It seems even more ironic, then, that whenever an owner wishes to dispose of an OTC call, the only portion of premium that can be salvaged is any *intrinsic value* the option may have acquired.

Exchange-traded calls, however, can be resold at any time. Their *time value* loss is limited to approximately that portion of total life the option was owned. Without this resale market for used calls and the ability to recover *time value,* which these new exchanges provide, it is doubtful that many investors would or should be interested in buying or selling options.

CBOE's Birth Brings New Life to Options—Because nearly every OTC call was different in striking price and expiration date from every other option, the only means of reselling them was through a kind of "want ad" approach, illustrated by Figure 2.

The first organization to recognize this situation and to do something to improve it was the Chicago Board of Trade. The securities-industry establishment apparently was quite surprised when the Board announced an extensive feasibility study with new methods for creating an option exchange. The Chicago Board of Trade is the world's largest market for trading future contracts in agricultural commodities, but at that time had no experience in securities.

Standardization was essential for exchange trading. The Board of Trade study team solved this problem by adapting many of the successful features of their commodity exchange. Standardization was accomplished by limiting terminations to four dates per year. One or two rounded numbers, always divisible by five, were selected as striking prices. These were near the current stock price at the time the calls were created.

A series of options terminating on three of the four dates is always available. In this way the maximum life of any exchange-traded call is about nine months. Calls are created and existing

CALLS

PER 100 SHARES (PLUS TAX)
Subject to Prior Sale or Price Change

33½	AMER EXPRESS	34¾	OCT. 17	$287.50
14½	AMER MAIZE	19⅞	FEB. 4	137.50
20⅛	BABCCK & WIL	23	OCT. 28	112.50
24¾	CAMPBEL RDLK	30	OCT. 13	100.00
11¼	CHRYSLER	11⅞	JAN. 12	137.50
64	CONTL OIL	73	NOV. 17	137.50
44⅜	DOME MINES	47½	NOV. 3	287.50
48⅜	DIAMOND SHM	49⅛	SEPT. 26	325.00
24½	FRESNILLO	27⅛	JAN. 27	187.50
44⅝	FAIRCHILD CM	44⅝	OCT. 23	450.00
9⅞	GAF CORP	10½	5 MOS.	187.50
18½	HOBART MFG	24⅛	DEC. 22	137.50
26	INTL NICKEL	27	NOV. 17	187.50
15⅜	LONE STAR IN	16¾	5 MOS.	167.50
27⅛	MAYTAG	29½	9 MOS.	350.00
63⅜	MOORE McCOR	61	OCT. 27	887.50
27	NCR CORP	30⅞	OCT. 3	100.00
38	OWENS CORN	39½	NOV. 17	287.50
68⅞	PITTSTON	66	OCT. 20	725.00
27⅛	ROBINTECH	28¾	OCT. 23	225.00
21⅛	REYNOLDS MET	21⅛	SEPT. 26	137.50
19¾	RUCKER	23	DEC. 29	187.50
13⅜	SALEM CORP	15¾	5 MOS.	162.50
12¼	SOUTHERN CO	13½	11 MOS.	225.00
56¾	STALEY MFG	60¼	OCT. 2	425.00
13	SUNSHINE MIN	17	5 MOS.	137.50
19¼	UV IND	22⅞	5 MOS.	137.50
13	UNIV OIL PRD	15¼	5 MOS.	162.50
52⅛	UNITED TECH	52¾	OCT. 20	387.50

PUTS

33½	AMER EXPRESS	33⅝	OCT. 20	$350.00
51⅞	AMAX	51	5 MOS.	587.50
24¾	CAMPBEL RDLK	25½	6 MOS.	387.50
37½	COMSAT	33¾	NOV. 11	137.50
22⅝	CROCKER INTL	26⅝	DEC. 22	525.00
20½	DIAMOND M D	21⅜	6 MOS.	350.00
44⅜	DOME MINES	44⅜	5 MOS.	787.50
85	EXXON	88⅜	OCT. 28	525.00
41¾	GEN DYNAMIC	43½	OCT. 8	450.00
94¾	HUGHES TOOL	96¾	3 MOS.	787.50
180¼	I B M	178¾	5 MOS.	1775.00
180¼	I B M	177½	3 MOS.	1075.00
84½	KERR MCGEE	85½	3 MOS.	687.50
50	MARSH MCLEN	54½	DEC. 1	787.50
85¼	PROCTER & GM	96	OCT. 28	1275.00
44¾	PHILLIP MOR	43⅞	3 MOS.	387.50
21⅛	REYNOLDS MET	21	4 MOS.	187.50
38¼	ROSARIO RES	37	NOV. 3	250.00
56¾	STALEY MFG	60	OCT. 2	687.50

THOMAS, HAAB & BOTTS
269-8100 — Toll Free 800-221-7093
50 Broadway, N.Y.C.
Mbrs. Chicago Board Options Exchange
Mbrs. Put & Call Brokers & Dealers Assn.

Figure 2. *A typical "want ad" for OTC options.*

ones retired according to changing conditions of supply and demand. As the price of the underlying stock moves away from established striking prices, a new set of options can be created for an existing series, leaving those with higher or lower striking prices unaffected.

CBOE is justifiably proud of five major improvements they have made in the field of securities options. In their words, these are:

1. "*Standardization* of securities option contracts and trading practices." (We have examined this feature several times so far.)

2. "*Continuous public reporting* of options transaction prices and volume via a last sale tape and electronic inquiry units." (Your broker has continuous access to this data and closing transactions are published in several newspapers.)

3. "*Appointment of market-makers* who have an obligation to help maintain a fair and orderly market in each listed option contract." (CBOE Market-Makers' function is to match buy and sell orders, but in a different, more competitive way than the private specialists who perform a similar function on AMEX and NYSE.)

4. "*Assumption of comprehensive self-regulatory responsibility* over option dealings on the exchange." (We have noted the problems that existed when regulatory responsibility was nonexistent in the old OTC option contracts.)

5. "*Provision of a Clearing Corporation* to streamline the processing of option trades and to strengthen the financial protections that stand behind option contracts." (Details are too extensive to describe here. They are completely explained in the Options Clearing Corporation Prospectus, which should be read before you start to invest in options.)

At the time CBOE requested SEC permission to organize this new type of market, the Commission expressed some concern about possible harmful side effects to other security markets. CBOE's obvious success, and the clamor of stock exchanges for permission to follow CBOE's lead, must have helped to assure SEC that option exchanges were a sound concept.

SEC's initial approval for CBOE was provisional. Then, before allowing CBOE to expand and operate on a more permanent basis, SEC required CBOE to agree to assist AMEX, PBW and any other exchanges that might wish to enter the option business in the future. This requirement was fulfilled by standardization of most option-trading procedures and formation of a jointly owned holding company, The Options Clearing Corporation. Its Prospectus and reporting system serves all option exchanges.

This benefits individual investors by sparing them the tremendous confusion that would have occurred had each exchange followed different procedures.

Certificateless Trading—This is a common feature of all option exchanges. It may be an unfamiliar arrangement to anyone not acquainted with a margin account. Fancy certificates or receipts are not issued for exchange-traded options. An entirely adequate broker's confirmation is your evidence of an option transaction.

Certificateless trading, once it is understood, is more of an advantage to the individual than to the broker. Option life is relatively short. The expense and risk to individuals of transmitting and holding a certificate, and then perhaps even overlooking the expiration dates, has been wisely eliminated.

Commissions—All option exchanges have a similar base scale of minimum commissions. However, actual transaction costs are not necessarily identical on different exchanges, or with different brokers. Currently these are as follows:

(1) Orders for the Purchase or Sale of a Single Option

Money Involved in the Order	Basic Commission
$ 100–2,499	1.3% + $12
2,500–4,777	0.9% + $22
4,778–30,000	$65

(2) Orders for the Purchase or Sale of Multiple Options (except that the basic commission per single option within a

multiple option order shall not be more than the rate specified in (1) above)

Money Involved in the Order	Basic Commission
$ 100–2,499	1.3% + $12
2,500–19,999	0.9% + $22
20,000–30,000	0.6% + $82

Plus:

First to tenth option covered by the order: $6 per option
Eleventh option and over covered by the order: $4 per option

The minimum commission for a single option involving $100 or more is $25. Closing transactions may be negotiated at a lower figure where the total value is under $100.

AMEX currently follows this schedule, except that on orders under $5,000, these commissions are increased by 10%, and over $5,000 by 15%. In addition, any other percentage surcharges which may apply to AMEX stock transactions (currently 8%) also apply to AMEX option commissions.

Earlier we looked under the hood at the option machinery. We saw that this is a vehicle that can be rented from CBOE and AMEX, the Hertz and Avis respectively of options, and also from PHLX.

You are now ready to look at your option compass and see which direction has the most to offer—but first you will need road maps. Let's look at these next and try to decide which investment direction and option routes may best meet your present needs.

Just as soon as you become familiar with the "maps," we will be ready to let CBOE, AMEX and PHLX "Put You in the Driver's Seat."

5

Option Road Maps Show the Way

Before mapping out option routes you should understand something about the roads. As you probably have already discovered in the world of stocks, there are no smooth investment expressways. This is even more true of options. In fact, if option routes are paved, it is only with good intentions! Some are well traveled and hard-surfaced, but none will be free of rough spots all the way.

This should warn you that market climate is very critical when you travel the option route. Although you need to be prepared to face storms that can mire you down in financial disaster, there also are many sunny days for exhilarating and profitable experiences when you travel along properly selected option routes.

Success is far more profitable if, before starting on an option journey, you try to make certain that the investment climate appears favorable for your specific trip. Advice of experts is useful, but do not be guided entirely by their predictions and opinions. Look around the scene, try to understand it, then make your own decisions. For instance, do you see clouds overlooked by the forecasters? Or is it possible the predicted storm is bypassing a specific option you have chosen?

The Conservative-Aggressive Direction—When you are ready to get behind the wheel of the option machine, your first trip should be a brief low-risk venture in familiar territory, a conservative-aggressive route. This is to say, you might purchase a low-premium call on a stock you believe will do especially well during the next few months. You will, of course, make every effort to select a highly profitable option. But then, if you don't succeed initially, console yourself by recognizing that quick-and-easy success the first time out is not necessarily in your best long-term interest. If you are not fortunate the first time, it may help you avoid overconfidence, thereby encouraging you to develop a more cautious attitude in the future. Let us hope it won't discourage you from trying again.

There are a number of sound, conservative reasons for taking the option route when making an initial purchase of a company's stock, rather than buying it outright.

You may feel a little uncertain about how this favorite stock will perform in the overall market climate you foresee immediately ahead. Yet, despite a general concern about market climate, you do have confidence that this particular stock is a winner. You do not want to miss a probable advance in its price, so you decide to buy one or more of its calls.

The stock price advances. What happens next? You will have enjoyed a gain in dollars about the same as though you had bought the stock. The only added option expense would be the relatively small amount you paid for the call's time value, perhaps 1 to 2% of the stock price per month.

Then what happens next when you still own the call, its market value is considerably greater than your cost, and it is about to expire? You now face a second decision, because there are two ways to take the profit. One way to is exercise the call, buy the stock at the option's striking price, much below the price it is currently trading on the NYSE, and hold it as an investment.

There is a second way to take the profit. If you have changed your mind about the stock, or for any other reason do not care to exercise the call, you simply tell your broker to sell it. Your gain on the option should be almost as great as the profit you would have made by purchasing the underlying stock, yet you would not have had as many dollars at risk, or paid as many dollars in commissions, on this option route.

Here is still another route you may find useful, if you have investments which are now frozen but will become liquid later, or which you do not wish to disturb at this time. For example, you may own Treasury bills or notes, certificates of deposit, discount bonds, mortgages, stock in a closely held corporation or one with a high capital-gains tax liability. Suddenly the stock market looks good to you. You would like to move out of the storm shelter onto the scenic route of common stocks, but do it without immediately liquidating these other investments.

You could take this route simply by purchasing calls on those optionable stocks which you would buy if you were more liquid. Premium cost—about 10% of the stock price for six-month calls. This is the way you could, in effect, convert frozen assets into an equivalent dollar-value equity position. Your cost for six months would be approximately equal to the annual interest received from the debt securities—yet they would not be disturbed. Result—about the same upside profit you would have enjoyed if all fixed investments were liquidated and their proceeds invested in the stocks. Maximum downside risk—limited to the option premiums, approximately the same as the probable annual income from the frozen investments.

Variations and details of these and other conservative-aggressive option routes will be explained further in Chapter 6.

The Conservative-Defensive Direction—The second direction we should explore on the option route map is conservative-defensive. Although Chapter 12 will discuss it in detail, let's first see what it is and why anyone might want to travel over such a route.

This is a course directly opposite the one we have just considered. Instead of buying options, you sell them. Going in a conservative-defensive direction, however, you would sell an option only if you owned the underlying stock. It can be a stock you now own or one that you purchase simultaneously with your sale of the call.

This conservative-defensive direction is one which uses stock options to produce instant income. For many investors, both individual and institutional, this may be the only option route ever taken.

Investors have sold OTC options for more than a century. These sellers were referred to as writers—a logical term because the seller wrote an option contract on a piece of paper and sold it to the second party. The term "writer" is still used when referring to the seller of options, but it is less appropriate now for a standardized exchange-traded option contract.

The procedure for selling a call is quite simple—just the opposite of that used to buy one. You don't pay a premium—you receive one, payable immediately in cash less a small commission.

Chapter 13 analyzes factors that determine the amount of premium you will pay or receive as a buyer or seller. For a brief introductory view, however, we will merely assume that the premium for a six-month call is equal to 10% of the market price of the stock.

Let's begin with an example which assumes that you own a few hundred shares of U.S. Steel stock with a current market price of $50 a share. AMEX options, with an expiration date about six months in the future, are quoted at $5. This means that your broker can sell a six-month call on 100 shares of your U.S. Steel stock for about $500. The commission would be about $25, so immediately you would receive about $475 net for each call you sold. You also would be entitled to receive all cash dividends payable during the life of the option.

One other mechanical detail should be explained. When you sell options on your stock, the certificate of ownership must be deposited with your broker. In the language of the trade, it will be held in "street name." This is necessary because the purchaser may exercise the call at any time and your broker must be in a position to deliver the stock without waiting for you to deliver it to him. Then, too, brokers cannot afford to take the chance that a seller might renege on his obligation. A broker would be taking this risk if the seller's stock certificate, or an equivalent amount of his cash, were not on deposit to back up endorsement of the option contract. Of course, the broker has no discretion in any event. Federal regulations and Options Exchange rules make this deposit mandatory.

It is easy to sell a call and collect instant income along with the regular dividends. The basic decision is whether or not to sell calls, and we will examine this subject at greater length in a later chapter.

For the writer of an exchange-traded call, termination also offers a choice of several alternatives. Since some are new opportunities, never having been available to the writer of OTC calls, it is worth taking time to understand them in order to choose the one best suited for your position under various conditions.

Each call you sell will terminate in one of three ways:

· You can buy back the call at any time before it is exercised by paying the current premium and a commission. This may be more or less than the premium received when you sold the call.

· If the market price of the stock is below the striking price when the call expires, the option is worthless. You need to do nothing. Your obligation to deliver stock will terminate with the call.

· A call you have sold which is in the money late in its life will undoubtedly be exercised. In that event your broker will sell the stock at the call's striking price, less a commission on the stock sale.

Assume that you either have the stock free of any option obligation or the proceeds from its sale. You are now in a position to sell another call on the same stock, or on a different stock using the proceeds of the previous transaction.

Option income you receive by repetition of this procedure, selling, for example, two six-month calls each year, should provide about 20% premium income, plus 5% in cash dividends for a total annual return of nearly 25% on your investment.

Of course, there is always the possibility that the market price of the stock may decline after the option is sold, and remain at a low level until after the option terminates. In this case the seller will still own the stock, but its market value would be less than when the option was sold.

If this happens, you may consider that the option premium helped to offset part or all of this decline in stock value—protection you would not have enjoyed had you merely continued to hold the stock. Premiums received from the sale of options are a form of insurance against the first decline of approximately 10% in market value of the underlying stock.

Whether you consider premiums received as instant income or insurance on stock, or both, many fascinating routes are available for you to travel along a conservative-defensive option direction. Chapter 7 will explore them more thoroughly.

Hedge Opt'ing—A third option direction on your investment

map leads to hedge opt'ing, if I may coin a phrase. Hedge opt'ing is a motorized investment steeplechase, a game of skill and chance where you keep the right foot on the accelerator and the left foot on the brake! There are ways to protect yourself and enjoy the advantages of traveling this way. These methods will be more understandable after gaining confidence in your ability to travel in those first two directions, as you will when you read more about them in Chapters 6 and 7.

In conventional option language, this hedge opt'ing is known as "spreading." It is the simultaneous purchase and sale of calls on the same stock, similar but with either different striking prices or expiration dates. Countless opportunities for a variety of conservative option hedges are available to help implement many kinds of short-term investment ideas.

Any further explanation of hedge opt'ing will be deferred until Part IV, so we can now move on to take a fast look at our fourth and last major direction.

The Speculative-Bearish Direction—This fourth major option strategy can best be described as a zigzag path through a live minefield. In no way is it conservative unless you have become a professional "sapper."

The vehicle that takes you into this investment minefield is the naked call—definitely a speculative-bearish way to go. A naked call receives its name from the fact that it is an option sold short, with no stock or other option held by the seller for protection in the event the underlying stock price advances substantially.

Consider this: When you buy a stock or option, you can never lose more than the amount you have paid. When you sell a stock or call short with no hedge, however, your potential loss is unlimited. This is reflected in the homey old adage attributed to the famous speculator Jim Livermore: "He who sells what isn't hizzun, must buy it back or go to prizzun."

With options, unlike stock, this is only true if the underlying stock is higher than the striking price when the call expires. If the stock is selling below the striking price when the call expires, no buy-back is necessary.

But selling naked calls can leave you stripped, as the title of Chapter 20 suggests, although there have been many occasions when an option seller traveling this direction has made a fortune. The route certainly is not for the faint of heart, but, as we shall see in Chapter 20, selling naked calls can be profitable in a bear market and this method has some advantages over others used on those occasions.

This brief overview of the option way and its four basic directions is designed to give you a perspective of the entire field of exchange-traded option call opportunities. Some investors may use only one of these, while others will take advantage of two or three or perhaps all four routes at various times and under different market conditions.

If you're ready, let's warm up your option engine and "Put You in the Driver's Seat" by first making some long calls.

PART II

Buying Calls

Calling in a Conservative-Aggressive Direction

6

Route 1: The Alternative Way

It seems logical to travel first in a conservative-aggressive direction while learning option ways. We can identify at least six different option routes that all lead in this direction. Which one shall we take? Later you may select a combination of several of these routes, but until you become more familiar with the option mode of investment travel, let's take them one at a time.

Chapter 5 suggested that options could be used as an alternative to direct equity investment. This may be the situation if your portfolio consists mainly of frozen assets, just at a time when the stock market is turning from bearish to bullish. You have a strong urge to invest immediately in blue-chip stocks, but, for any one of several possible reasons, you are unwilling or unable to liquidate and convert these assets into stock.

Assume, for example, that you own a $10,000 Treasury bill. Now you would like to be invested in 200 shares of AT&T common stock during the next six months, without cashing the T bill.

You could accomplish this simply by purchasing two Telephone calls. AT&T calls usually have about the lowest time value premium of any comparable options, so your cost for two six-month calls (on 200 shares) would be about $600 ($300 each), when both the stock and striking price are at $45.

Now let's assume that six months and a few days later, AT&T stock trades at $54½ on the NYSE and you decide to sell your calls. How much profit would you make? With 9½ points of intrinsic value, the premium now would be at least $950 for each, or $1,900. After deducting the $600 premium and $85 in commissions, you would realize a net gain of $1,200. This is equivalent to 200% on your premium, an annual rate of 400%, made possible by an increase of only 15% in the price of the underlying AT&T stock.

Long-term capital-gain tax rates would apply. Had the stock and option values declined, the option could have been resold to recapture a part of the premium. If this were done while the calls had been held for less than six months, the loss would have been short term.

You could, if you wished, exercise the calls by purchasing Telephone stock, rather than sell them for a $1,200 net gain. Your cost basis for 200 shares would be $9,600, even though the stock had a market value of $10,900 at that time. It is interesting to note that your maximum risk (exposure to loss) while owning the calls never exceeded about one year's interest on a $10,000 Treasury bill.

Of course, the Telephone stock in our example could have gone down instead of up. What then? This leads directly to the second option way in the conservative-aggressive direction— Route 2: The Insured Way.

7

Route 2: The Insured Way

Options can be a form of investment insurance. This statement may seem questionable if you believe, as many do, that options are always the highest-risk security in the investment market.

Call premiums, like premiums paid for casualty or term life insurance are, of course, a wasting asset. However, each does provide the function of protecting against risk of some future unfavorable event. A call affords two-way protection—when the stock goes up and when it goes down. In this way it might be said to resemble an endowment policy, which pays off whether you live or die.

A call protects against being out of the market and missing a stock-price increase. It also protects against a drop in price by strictly limiting maximum loss to the premium cost.

Whenever there is a stock that you feel optimistic about and would like to buy, but decide not to do so until later, you have taken a risk. If the stock price advances, you will pay considerably more when you finally do buy it. Purchase of a call at the time you first recognize the opportunity protects you against the risk of paying a higher price during the whole life of the call.

The second form of protection provided by a call is similar to automobile collision insurance. It protects against casualty loss. The call premium is similar to a collision-insurance premium. With each you buy protection. Should your favorite stock become a casualty for any reason, due to some surprising development that reduces its market value—such as lower earnings, huge write-offs, new competition, unfavorable rumors or news, anything—your loss is limited to the premium, and not necessarily all of that. You receive this protection because the person who sold the call was willing to take all the remaining losses in excess of your premium.

Let's look again at the example used on Route 1. For simplicity, assume that the $10,000 is cash in a checking account, and look for an answer to the question "Would purchase of those two AT&T calls have reduced your risk?"

Of course, we must start with the assumption that one of our investment goals is to enjoy benefits which we anticipate will be realized through ownership of 200 shares of AT&T stock. In other words, we are unwilling to risk being without this investment protection during the next few months. The basic decision, then, is whether to buy 200 shares of stock for $9,000 or two calls for $600.

Now let's compare relative downside risks of each choice. Assume that instead of advancing 9½ points, the stock declined by that amount. Under these conditions your $9,000 investment in stock would be worth only $7,100, a loss of $1,900. The calls cost $600 and would have very little value now, but they did protect against the additional $1,300 loss you would have suffered by going the direct stock route.

Whether you buy a call or a collision-insurance policy, you pay a premium, but you know exactly the extent of your maximum loss under even the most unfavorable circumstances. Your protection derives from another person or firm that covers your call or policy, and insures you against additional losses by absorbing them as required in their contractual obligation.

The only reason for buying a collision policy is to protect against casualty loss. However, this is merely the secondary purpose in purchasing a call. The primary reason is to protect against the risk of not making a capital gain through ownership of a specific stock. Buyers of calls are well aware of this primary motive, but fewer seem to evaluate or even recognize this important secondary protection against substantial loss.

The term "insurance poor" can apply to option protection as well as any other kind. How much should you buy? Some or all of your option premium occasionally will be lost, just as the premium is always lost when you buy a term life or casualty insurance policy and live, or don't have an accident. It would be foolhardy, or worse, to use most of your net worth (in our example, to use the entire $10,000) for the purchase of calls, as it would be to use all your net worth to buy a six-month term life-insurance policy.

You have seen how the value of a call moves up or down ten to twenty times faster than its underlying stock. When you buy calls for their insurance characteristic, it is a good rule to buy calls on no more shares then you would otherwise purchase outright.

You probably have some figure in mind as the maximum total commitment that you can dedicate to equity investments. To travel Route 2 in the conservative-aggressive direction you should add these calls to your other stock investments on the basis of the value of their underlying stock price, rather than the amount of the call premium. There is an immediate minimum penalty for violation of this rule: Your status is automatically shifted from investor to speculator!

Route 2: The Insured Way can be used alone or in combination with other option ways to reduce risk when you travel in a conservative-aggressive direction. The premium cost for this protection is relatively modest. Like automobile insurance, it protects you by limiting loss to a known and acceptable maximum.

Under the anticipated favorable conditions, however, a call premium buys high leverage. This leverage resembles that of the premium compared with face amount or death value of a term life-insurance policy. Of course, the desires and expectations are vastly different for a call than for term life insurance. Successful call leverage creates a happy, even euphoric situation. Fortunately for both types of protection, the probability of a call's being exercised and settled profitably is much, much greater, too.

For all the benefits along Routes 1 and 2, you might expect compensating disadvantages, such as higher commissions or other operating expenses. To investigate this possibility we now turn right to Route 3: The Thrifty Way.

8

Route 3: The Thrifty Way

Your previous experience must have demonstrated that in the security world there are no continuously smooth expressways to speed you along toward your investment goals, and on even the roughest of these roads a toll is charged. What, then, is the thriftiest way to travel?

With the deregulation of brokers' commissions in May 1975, it is no longer possible to use commission figures which apply to all firms. For our examples we will use the last fixed minimum commissions published. These may be a little lower or higher than those in effect with your broker now.

Let's start by referring again to the AT&T example used in previous chapters. Your commission on the purchase of 200 shares of AT&T stock bought for $45 per share would be about $170. Shares sold later at $54½ would incur commission expense of slightly over $200.

Commissions to purchase two AT&T calls would be less than $35, and after their appreciation, $50 to resell. Should they become worthless there would, of course, be no resale commission.

Compare the tolls for each route. Round-trip commissions on 200 shares of AT&T stock would total about $370, equal to six months of dividends on this high-income stock. It is also four to ten times the round-trip commission of $35 to $85 for a similar journey on Route 3: The Thrifty Way option route.

Any investor with surplus liquid assets will not need to use Route 1: The Alternative Way. Then, assuming there is no concern about risking a price decline, Route 2: The Insured Way would not be of much interest. Those investors who are determined to stay with their present stock holdings for several years, during good and bad times, could hardly care less about Route 3: The Thrifty Way. However, if you are neither terribly affluent nor indifferent about taking unnecessary risks nor oblivious to investment expense, you may be interested in ways to reduce transaction costs.

International Harvester, for example, is a stock that frequently looks very attractive and tempting. With Harvester calls trading on CBOE, an investor made a decision to purchase a call instead of the stock at $34. It was an in-the-money call and the premium of $600 represented four points of intrinsic value over its $30 striking price. Then, only a few days later, the stock went dead and its price started down. The call was sold immediately and $550 of the premium was recovered. Total loss, including two commissions, was $100.

Compare this modest cost with the probable outcome of the alternative route—purchase of the stock. Commissions for purchase and sale of the stock would have been over $125. But the stock price had dropped 1¼ points while the option was being held, so total loss on the stock route would probably have been $250 ($125 and $125) or more, 2½ times greater.

There is another thrift point illustrated by this example, an intangible option benefit but one that is perhaps even more important. Most investors find it is psychologically more difficult to immediately admit and correct large mistakes in judgment than it is to correct smaller ones.

High round-trip commission expense on stocks can also cause an investor to hesitate before taking a relatively large initial loss when the stock price drops soon after the purchase. This tempts one to stay invested longer at the risk of compounding the problem.

How much loss did this investor avoid by taking Route 3: The Thrifty Way? In this actual example Harvester stock subsequently fell to $17. Had the investor bought stock at $34, rather than a call, it might have been held to this point and then sold with a loss of over $1,700.

Because commissions on options are so much lower than for an equivalent number of shares of common stock, you can often save money by testing the water before jumping in all the way. A trial run can be more economical and less likely to create large losses if you will use Route 3 when you are not sure of the stock's immediate future.

The idea of using a call as a thrifty way to begin the possible acquisition of a new stock position may be compared to a rental with an option to buy a home. If you were given the choice of buying a home outright or first leasing it with an option to buy, you probably would never choose to buy first, especially if there was no moving expense. Low-cost rental with an option to buy would avoid the possibility of being locked into a position in which you were unhappy, and if you chose to move out, it would, in effect, save two large real-estate commissions.

You may seldom, if ever, have an opportunity for trial occupancy of a home before buying, but you do have a wide variety of similar choices in acquiring stocks through purchase of options. When the public begins to understand the advantages of the option Thrift Way to cost reduction in acquiring equity positions, there should be a wild rush of investors to form trial marriages with their favorite stocks via this option route.

Cost of capital is by far the major long-term expense in owning stocks. If your stocks are held in a margin account this percentage is apparent because it is shown on your broker's statement each month. Cost of capital is not the same for all investors, but your cost must be at least equal to the rate of interest or total return on money you could be receiving if your funds were in some alternative investment.

On Route 1 we examined one facet of using options to minimize capital cost in acquiring stock when you have frozen assets. Capital cost, either for interest paid out or not received, is nearly always ten times greater per dollar of equity controlled than the cost to obtain the same position by holding one of the stock's calls.

The key to lower capital costs on Route 3 is to compare the monthly price you would pay for the time value of a call with the total return you are currently receiving on your own capital—let's say it is about 12%. Then, for example, if you are interested in a specific option and its time value is less than 1% per month (12% per year) it would be attractive for its low capital cost, along with all its other probable advantages.

Sometimes you may be in a hurry to reach a destination. You are willing to take more risk if doing so promises to get you there sooner. When those occasions arise in your investment life you can take Route 4: The Speed Way.

9

Route 4: The Speed Way

Buying calls is the Speed Way to gains in the investment world. To reach your profit goals quickly there is no faster way to go. It is an aggressive method, but whether it is also conservative is questionable. The answer to this depends largely on the individual's stock market and option experience, knowledge of the specific company and the action of its stock.

In Chapter 6 (Route 1: The Alternative Way) it was indicated that an investor who bought calls on more shares than he was capable of owning outright was in danger of becoming a speculator. So be it. There is nothing wrong in being a speculator, *as long as the individual understands the potential risks and is in a position to accept them without disastrous consequences.*

After an option trader has gained a reasonable amount of experience, it should be possible to move to a more speculative position without necessarily forfeiting a conservative standing. The secret is to use the power and speed of option leverage in a controlled conservative way, as illustrated in several of the previous examples.

For another actual illustration, typical of leverage provided by calls, consider this one on Bethlehem Steel. At a time when the stock was selling for $27, its $25 calls were $4. Five calls were purchased for $2,000. This was $700 less than 100 shares of the stock would have cost. Within two months the stock rose to $34 and the calls advanced from $4 to $12. The total value of the five calls increased from $2,000 to $6,000. With less invested than the price of 100 shares of stock (but with considerably more risk), the option premiums appreciated $4,000, or 200%, compared with an increase of $700 or 25% for the stock.

Later BS stock fell back to 27½. In addition to the $25 calls, there were also some $30 calls, 2½ points out of the money. With just seven weeks of life remaining, they were traded at only ½, or 50¢ a share. Then, in two weeks, Bethlehem stock again advanced, this time by six points. The $30 calls leaped from ½ to 3¾, a gain of 650% in only ten trading days. Also, the $25 calls which had fallen back to 2¾ (little more than their intrinsic value) advanced to 8½, a smaller but still respectable gain of 224%.

A dramatic movement in IBM calls was described in Chapter 2. You may remember that the April $220 calls advanced 258% in one week. These had been trading at just $1. Theoretically a trader could have put $16,300 (the price of 100 shares of IBM stock) into the purchase of 16,300 of these calls and watched it grow to $45,520 in only five trading days. Then, in only three more weeks, these calls traded at 12½, a gain of 1250%. Theoretically, and *only* theoretically, a speculative investment of $16,300 in these IBM calls would have increased to over $200,000 in three weeks. That same dollar investment in IBM stock increased during the period from $16,300 to $22,012—a much smaller gain.

Obviously no one bought 16,300 of these calls. The open interest, or total number of the calls outstanding, was only 4,348. Some traders, however, did profit by this IBM price advance because 1,603 April 220's were sold at $1 during the week prior to this move. Even late-comers who bought 5,674 of the calls after that first big week must have made gains of 268% in many instances.

How does one recognize such situations soon enough to take advantage of them? The first requirement, of course, is that you must correctly understand the current and probable future price trend of the underlying stock. To do this consistently, there is no substitute for stock market knowledge and experience, either your own or your investment adviser's, or both. It is not necessary that your knowledge extend to the entire stock market. It may be limited to a small group of stocks. Since option exchanges offer such a wide variety of calls on the nation's highest quality blue-chip stocks, you may choose to follow only a few groups and ignore the others.

One thing is certain. If a stock you like is in a strong price uptrend, the option values will follow. If the striking price is near the stock price, it will always move up almost dollar for dollar and at about ten times the percentage rate as the stock. Of course, when the stock price trend reverses, the call premiums also will fall at a much greater percentage rate than the stock.

Once you decide to purchase options on a specific stock, how do you determine which ones to buy? Suggestions to help you evaluate the advantages of different time periods and striking prices are given in Chapter 12. Whether to buy long-term, short-term, in-the-money or out-of-the-money calls, and how far in or out, will depend on the individual's situation and his immediate goals. As previous examples have demonstrated, there are wide variations in percentage price movements, even with only slightly different calls on the same stock.

Bernard Baruch, America's best-known and perhaps most successful speculator, made it a rule never to become involved in any speculative venture until he had mastered all the facts. He proved that successful speculation was not luck, but rather an infinite capacity for taking pains—the pains to analyze all available facts with courage, persistence, and judgment unclouded by emotion. He surely would have made an even greater fortune had exchange-traded options with their Speed Way to gains been available in his time.

To take advantage of the great inherent leverage of options, it is necessary to utilize their unusual trading flexibility. This suggests that to be successful you should regularly watch market trends and be prepared to make rapid decisions to buy or sell your calls at a favorable time and price.

Prospective option speculators may correctly view calls as "Flexible Flyers." However, options have a conservative kind of flexibility because they make it possible to change investment direction quickly and economically while en route. We will become more familiar with this flexibility as we move on to Route 5: The Flexible Way.

10

Route 5: The Flexible Way

A common stock alone does not offer much flexibility. If you do not own it you have two choices—buy it or don't buy it. After you own it there are still only two ways to go—hold on or sell.

An option has much greater flexibility at all times—when you buy it, while you own it and when you dispose of it.

Flexibility When You Buy—Multiple Striking Prices—Calls generally have several different striking prices and always more than one life span. Each of these variations has a different characteristic. A call far out of the money may sell for only pennies, and its value will change very little with ordinary price movement of the stock. However, should the stock price finally move up close to the striking price, the option can move 100% or more in a week, or even in a single day.

Other calls in the money may be available on the same stock. They will advance about dollar for dollar with the stock price and of course at a much higher percentage rate. When the stock price moves, these calls may have a lower percentage change than similar out-of-the-money options, but their dollar move will always be greater.

Take two or more calls with a common expiration date. Those with lower striking prices will require a higher premium investment, reflecting their greater intrinsic value. Those with higher striking prices will generally have a higher time value, if they are not too far out of the money. However, the probability is much greater that they will expire out of the money and become worthless, while in-the-money calls generally return some premium dollars to the owner even if the stock declines.

A stock whose price has been very stable may have calls at only one striking price, while others whose price has fluctuated wildly over the past few months can have six or more sets of calls available at six different striking prices.

This opportunity to choose from among several striking prices is a unique flexibility among securities, one which permits you to fine-tune varying degrees of cost and risk against potential gains on a single stock with the risk-reward relationships determined by the public-opinion markets.

Flexibility When You Buy—Different Life Spans—Another reason for taking Route 5: The Flexible Way is the availability of calls with various life spans. This valuable feature is especially useful when you are interested in owning a stock only for a few months. Perhaps you believe that substantially higher stock earnings or an increased dividend will be announced soon, or you anticipate a tender offer for the stock, a spin-off or any other favorable event.

Options permit the short-term "rental" of an equity position to match personal investment needs without forcing you to pay larger premiums for more time than you require, or the higher commissions for a short-term round-trip stock transaction. Options vis-à-vis stock purchases might be compared with paying for parking space by the hour or day, rather than having to pay for a full month every time you wish to leave your car.

Example of Price and Time Flexibility—This flexible way can be illustrated with another AT&T example. In the winter of 1975 AT&T warrants were outstanding for purchase of about 31 million shares of stock at $52 per share. They were to expire on May 15, 1975, but it was very clear to most investors that AT&T management was extremely hopeful that their stock would sell for more than $52 before May 15. Exercise of these warrants would generate $1.6 billion of badly needed new equity.

With announcement of a Government antitrust suit against AT&T, the stock immediately dropped into the low 40's. Then it came back to the mid-40's, and in January trading closed at $48½.

On January 31, with the stock at $48½, CBOE offered a choice of seven AT&T calls. Their closing prices were as follows:

Striking	Premiums		
Prices	*April*	*July*	*October*
$50	$ $^{15}/_{16}$	$1⅝	$2
45	3⅞	4¾	5½
40	8⅜	N.A.	N.A.

N.A.—No option available.

Would you have bought AT&T calls if you were as familiar with options then as you are now? If so, which ones?

A conservative investor would have chosen July or October calls, because April calls expired more than two weeks before the warrants terminated. On the other hand, a less conservative person might have purchased April calls. The rationale for this might be that if anything was going to happen which would push the stock over $52 and thereby cause warrants to be exercised, it would probably occur by the end of April. Also, by choosing these instead of Julys, one could buy nearly twice as many calls for the same premium dollars.

Like the queen in a game of chess, options can be moved horizontally to various time squares, vertically to different striking prices, and even diagonally in combinations of time and price. After you decide which time span you might choose, what about striking price? Would you choose the 50's? Were they a better buy than the 45's or 40's? Chapter 12 will offer guidelines to help answer these questions, but certain considerations may already be obvious.

If the stock price at the end of April was unchanged at $48½, the April 50's would be worthless while the 45's and 40's would sell at their intrinsic value, about 3½ and 8½ respectively. If the stock closed at $45 or below, the 45's and 50's would both be worthless and the 40's would have dropped to half or less of their January 31 value.

But, if AT&T stock advanced to $55, for example, the 50's would terminate with a premium of about $5, an increase of 400%. The 45's would sell for about $10, a gain of 150% and the 40's at $15 up 75%.

This example illustrates two kinds of inherent option flexibility, qualities which open up new application ideas for using this investment tool to meet a wide variety of individual investor attitudes and situations.

Flexibility During the Holding Period—Previous chapters have shown how relatively low dollar commissions on options make it feasible to terminate calls quickly, whenever they have served their purpose.

Another flexibility is the way an option can serve as one leg of a hedged position, which you might create by selling a similar but not identical option on the same stock for the second leg.

Also, a call can be used to protect the short sale of a stock. Although these more complex option maneuvers will be explained in Chapters 17 and 18 they are mentioned here to further illustrate how option flexibility and adaptability can help you meet changed conditions, even after the call is purchased and before it is terminated.

Flexible Tax Treatment—Federal income-tax treatment of option trading has both interesting advantages and surprising problems. These, too, will be discussed later, but one advantage that applies to the purchase of calls is understandable now. The most distant option available on any stock always has more than six months of life. It can be held and then terminated for either short or long-term gains or losses at your discretion.

Flexibility at Termination—You have several choices in terminating an option. It can be resold or bought back at any time during regular market hours. An order may be entered at the market, or with a specific price limit. Your broker can describe other types of limit orders.

Then, of course, as the purchaser of a call you have the basic right to terminate it by exercising it at any time, converting the call into the underlying common stock at the striking price.

In Route 5: The Flexible Way, you have seen how options often can help you reach investment goals with greater precision by balancing invested assets and risk against probable gain and loss. Our next trip will be along Route 6: The Diversified Way. This will take you through beautiful blue-chip investment scenes, an elite area of the security world in which you may have thought you could never afford to travel.

11

Route 6: The Diversified Way

Quality stocks may seem out of reach for many investors who avoid the well-known blue-chip stocks because of their relatively high price per share. Options now make it possible for any investor to "rent" the bluest of blue chips regardless of their market price.

Investors who do not trade in odd lots (less than 100 shares) would not ordinarily own IBM in a well-diversified portfolio unless their net worth was in six figures. However, with options now available on IBM, and about 200 other blue-chip stocks, anyone can acquire a temporary interest in 100 shares of the most expensive stock for an investment of only a few hundred dollars.

Not that everyone, or anyone, should immediately acquire such options—but when conditions are right to take a position in high-quality issues, options do provide a short-term way to do so with relatively little capital.

Of course, options on high-quality stocks are no more risk-free than options on any other stocks. As we mentioned earlier, when you buy options on stocks you could not afford to own outright, you are acting more like a speculator than like a conservative-aggressive investor.

Diversification By Industry—Options on leading stocks in nearly every major U.S. industry are now available. When you think of buying an option, if you do not have a valid reason for choosing one particular stock, it is wise to look first at broad industry groups that seem most favorably situated for the immediate future. After determining which group or groups seem well situated, you can then make a selection of a specific company based on whatever technical or fundamental analysis you prefer.

Companies which have exchange-traded options are tabulated in Appendix A, arranged by industry. This list and related data are not current and are included only to indicate the type of information which, if updated, might be useful to have before you select a stock option to buy.

For example, in the data processing and copying industries, in addition to IBM, options are available on CBOE for Honeywell, Sperry Rand and Xerox; and on AMEX, calls are traded on Digital Equipment and Burroughs.

In the petroleum and natural gas industries, you may choose from among Atlantic Richfield, EXXON, Kerr McGee, Mobil, Pennzoil, Tesoro and Standard of Indiana on CBOE; Gulf, Texaco, Mesa, Standard of California, Phillips and Tenneco on AMEX; and Amerada-Hess, Louisiana Land and Continental Oil on PHLX. In industry after industry nearly all leaders are included on one of the four option exchanges.

Most of the capital gains enjoyed by U.S. investors during the past 25 years have been achieved on stocks whose calls are currently traded on these option exchanges. Some of them may disappoint their owners in the next 25 years while others will continue to grow at an above-average rate. Two things about these companies are worth remembering. First, they have been carefully selected, with SEC approval, to meet rigid conservative criteria. Secondly, they include most of America's largest and wealthiest corporations.

Diversification by Stock Market Characteristics—Options also provide a means to diversify among a selection of stocks with various degrees of growth in earnings and price, and with high or low price-earnings ratios. If you want to buy some options which are considered most likely to give rapid price movement, you might choose stocks with a history of wide price fluctuations. These stocks are often referred to as having a high Beta Factor, and their calls generally have a higher premium. Options on stocks which historically have had a relatively narrow price movement usually have a relatively lower premium. A diversified portfolio would probably include both types.

To illustrate—a six-weeks call on conservative AT&T may cost less than 4% of the stock price, while a similar call on McDonald's would be over 8%.

Diversification among stocks with widely different P/E (price-earnings) ratios is another way to travel along Route 6's Diversified Way in a conservative-aggressive direction. When investors expect corporate earnings to increase, for example, stocks with high P/E ratios often advance more rapidly than stocks whose earnings are capitalized at a much lower rate.

On the other side of this coin, when earnings are in a general decline, stocks with a high P/E ratio are the ones most often sold short by professionals in the belief that high P/E stocks are likely to decline faster than stocks with low P/E ratios. In a bear market an investor with a diversified option portfolio might lighten his holdings of calls on stocks with high P/E ratios or eliminate them entirely. In a definite bull market calls on stocks with high P/E's would generally be preferred.

The most important stock market characteristic for every investor or speculator to identify is whether or not the overall market is in a bullish or bearish trend. In a broad bull market, owners of a diversified and thoughtfully chosen group of options should almost always realize attractive gains. On the other hand, in a broad bear market there is hardly any way to select and purchase a diversified group of calls which will not have substantial losses.

There are ways, however, to use options profitably in a bear market. This additional example of option diversification will be considered in later chapters because it involves selling options and buying puts. Suffice it to say now, that diversified bear market strategies vary from the extremely conservative-defensive approach of writing calls against owned stock and buying puts to the very aggressive-speculative sale of naked calls.

Diversification by Option Characteristics—An option portfolio can be diversified by owning an assortment of options expiring in each of several time periods. If you believe that a stock is favorably positioned for an upward price move but you have no convictions as to when it might happen, you could buy calls in each of the three expiration months. Then, if the stock price advances quickly, your total gain would be a higher percentage of premium cost than if you had bought only the more distant calls. On the other hand, when you purchase only the shortest term calls and the move comes late, you may miss it entirely.

The purchase of calls at different striking prices is still another way to diversify. Lower striking-price calls are more likely to retain part of their premium value on stock declines, and they will gain more dollars on any price advance. However, higher striking-price calls have a lower dollar premium, will not lose as many dollars on a sharp decline in stock price, and will probably appreciate at a higher percentage rate on a stock advance. A diversified combination of calls at various striking prices could help balance the advantages and disadvantages of each.

Option-price relationships are confusing. You may wish to return to this chapter after you have read Chapter 12, "Guide Rails to Get You Started on the Right Track." Its five "rules of thumb" should help you locate the best option values before you start to buy.

12

Guide Rails to Get You Started on the Right Track

How will you know whether or not a call is fairly priced? Premiums are determined by an auction market, so they do represent a price at which supply and demand are in balance. But when you decide to buy, will you select a call whose premium represents good value for you?

Guides to Fair Premium Cost—With experience gained through actual option trading, you will acquire an instinctive judgment of option values. Ultimately this will serve as your best test of premium fairness and worth to you. But until you develop this judgment you may find it helpful to draw on the experience of others.

There are no firm pricing rules for options. However, by breaking down the premium into its major components, it is possible to assign a fair value for each and arrive at an acceptable total cost. Knowledge of six basic factors that influence premium prices will help you select the best option values. Only three need to be numerically evaluated, and with only the simplest mental arithmetic. These are capital cost, market risk, and stock volatility.

The guides which follow are derived empirically, based on extensive analysis of published transaction data. You can practice by testing them against current data in your newspaper until you feel comfortable using them, or make some new ones of your own.

If you should find a call premium which is priced far higher than any calculation would justify, don't discard it. This could be a great opportunity to sell a call at a very attractive high price.

Two-way investment flexibility is one of the great features of marketable options. They offer one of the few examples in business or finance where the only mark-up between wholesale and retail is in effect a relatively very small broker's commission, and where you can shift between these functions at will. Part III, which follows this chapter, explains how to sell options for instant income.

Value Guide for the Capital-Cost Component of Premium —To simplify an analysis of premium cost, first consider three elements of time value. We will start by examining only the shortest term calls with a remaining life of a few weeks to three months. After you acquire an understanding of the composition of these premiums, it will be easier to see how to adjust for the more distant calls.

As a further simplification, begin by assuming that in every instance the call striking price and the current market price of the stock are identical. Later you will see how to adjust for calls either in or out of the money, the more normal situation.

Our analysis of premium cost starts by recognizing that the person who sells you a call must be compensated for your use of his capital invested in the underlying stock. This is because the seller must be able to deliver the stock whenever you decide to call it. To do this he must lock up the stock or equivalent cash for the life of your call. The seller cannot know what the going rate of interest will be during the next six to nine months. As one guideline, many banks charge credit-card holders 1½% per month for short-term loans. The seller probably feels entitled to receive about that much to cover his capital cost component of the option you buy. Since he gives up all opportunity for capital gain on his stock, certainly a minimum capital charge of 1% per month seems reasonable.

Value Guide for the Market-Risk Component of Premium— The seller's total compensation must be greater than the maximum rate of credit-card bank interest, however, because much more risk is involved. For example, while he is holding underlying stock for your option, its price, or even the entire stock market, could collapse. As the buyer, you can walk away from it, but the seller cannot. As compensation for assuming market risks, the seller deserves, and usually should receive, an additional 1% of the striking price per month of option life.

The sum of these two components is about 2% per month times the stock price. Occasionally there may be small variations. For example, all cash dividends on stocks with marketable options belong to the stockholder, not to the option holder. When a significant dividend is to be paid during the life of the option, writers may take this into consideration and offer calls at a slightly lower premium than they might otherwise.

Although these two components of cost are stated as a per-cent per month, frequently options with a remaining life of sev-eral weeks to three months may have a minimum premium which is nearly flat for a time. This is, of course, only true as long as the stock remains steady and near the option striking price.

Value Guide for the Volatility Component—Some stock prices fluctuate much more than others. The measure of this characteristic is known as the Beta Factor of a stock. This com-pares the degree of fluctuation between a specific stock, and the New York Stock Exchange Composite Average, which has been given a Beta Factor of 1.0. Stocks with a Beta over 1.0 have fluctuated more than the NYSE Composite Average. Stocks with a Beta of less than 1.0 have been less volatile than the NYSE average. These are long-term comparisons, usually covering a trading period of two to five years, so Beta is not a measure of recent fluctuation. Although it may suggest the possible future relative volatility of the stock, and usually does influence option premium values, the Beta Factor is no guarantee of the direction, speed or amount of change to be expected in future option prices.

Beta Factor for each underlying stock is included in the Ap-pendix. Ratings change from time to time, so you should use only current sources of Beta data for premium evaluation.

Because a Beta higher than 1.0 indicates a stock history of greater-than-average price fluctuation, the seller's risk appears to be above normal, and the option will usually command a propor-tionally higher premium. A high Beta also encourages a belief that fluctuations will be upward, and so tends to make the buyer willing to pay more.

Five empirical rules have been formulated to give you some

feeling of what might be a nominal value of any call. Obviously not all calls will have premiums in accord with these rules. This can cause them to be either more or less attractive to you, but it should be worthwhile to understand in which direction a specific premium deviates from a nominal value.

It is very important to remember that rules 1, 2 and 3 apply only to calls that are almost exactly at the money—that is, the call striking price and the stock price are the same. Then Rule 4 suggests a way to adjust for an out-of-the-money call and Rule 5 for calls in the money.

Rule of Thumb Number One—The price of a short-term call (over one but less than three months) will be approximately equal to six times the price of one share of stock, multiplied by the stock's Beta Factor.

This formula reflects three major premium components:

   · 3% for the basic three-month capital cost (1% $\times$ 3 months)
   · 3% for general stock market risk, and
   · the Beta Factor reflecting long-term volatility of the underlying stock.

Three minor components may also affect the premium. They cannot be put into a formula, but should one of them become unusually significant it will cause a discrepancy between Rule One and the actual premium. These are:

   · Recent dramatic change in future prospects for the corporation and its stock.
   · Overall change in the total stock market trend, and
   · The supply and demand for a specific call.

The direction of any up or down effect on option premiums due to these three factors is quite obvious. The amount of deviation from the nominal evaluation derived from Rule One is also dependent on market emotion at the time. If you believe the market's response is correct, you will adjust your evaluation in line with popular opinion. If not, and if you are right, a contrary position in regard to premium value could be rewarding.

For example, premium time value is generally priced higher than normal in a strong bull market. When the overall market turns bearish, however, many options lose nearly all time value. Once this happens, and you believe the market will turn bullish well in advance of expiration dates on currently traded options, selective purchases can be made at bargain prices.

Not every stock will fit the formula of Rule One. A major reason is that Beta is based on long-term volatility, and may not reflect current price action or recent changes in stock popularity. Another consideration is that other investors may know or believe something of significance that you do not know or have not evaluated. If your judgment is very far out of line with the market, you may be looking at an unusual profit opportunity, if you are right.

Let's apply Rule One. On February 21, 1975, Ford stock closed at 34⅞. The April $35 call sold at 2¼. Was that a fair price? For capital cost and risk we multiply $35 by 6 and get $210. The Ford Beta Factor was 1.10, so we multiply $210 by 1.10 and arrive at a calculated premium of $231—as close to 2¼ as we should expect with any theoretical calculation.

Now try another example. On the same day Texas Instrument stock was selling for $80 a share and the April $80 call closed at 5¾. Six times $80 is $480, so the actual premium seems a bit high. But, wait a minute. What about Beta? TI's Beta is 1.25. Now 1.25 times $480 equals $600—close enough to 5¾ to have satisfied you of its fairness, had you been in the market for such a call that day.

Rule Number Two for the Midi-Term View—The premium for the midi-term (four to seven months) will be about 50% more than the corresponding short-term call.

For a quick check point you can also assume that: *The midi-term premium will seldom be less than the shorter term premium, plus 3% of the striking price.*

Let's try Ford and TI examples again, this time with the July premiums. On that same day the Ford July $35 call closed at 3½—exactly 50% more than the April call. This premium also met the second test. It was slightly above the figure called for by the shortcut for minimum cost—$225 + (3 times $35) or $330, slightly less than the $350 actual premium.

TI July $80 calls closed at 9⅛. The rule says that the April premium (5¾) plus 50% would make the theoretical premium 8⅝. The shortcut check is April premium plus 3% of $80. This equals only $815, or 8⅛. From these calculations it appears that the actual premium on the July calls may have been about ½ point too high. Was there any other evidence? How about relative volume? There were 304 April calls traded that day but only 13 July $80's. This suggests that the July calls may have been priced slightly higher than our rule called for, because of lack of interest in selling—or perhaps it was vice versa! With only 13 calls traded all day, it also is possible that the last trade was made early in the day when the stock and other calls were trading at higher prices.

The Longest-Term Fee Follows Rule Number Three—Premiums for the longest-term calls (seven to nine months) equal two times the premium of the corresponding shortest-term calls.

There is also a quick double-check point: *This premium will seldom be less than that of the shortest-term call, plus 6% of striking price."*

Let's return to the same Ford and TI examples. The Ford October $35 call closed at 4½—exactly twice the 2¼ April call price. The TI October $80 closed at 11½—exactly twice the 5¾ price at which the April call closed.

Obviously not all examples will fit the formula quite this precisely, but it is surprising that so many do. When options have nearly a full 3, 6 and 9 months of life remaining, premiums generally should be a little higher than calculated. As call life diminishes to approach 1, 4 and 7 months, premiums should be a little lower. Variations of ¼ or ½ point, more or less, are to be expected.

*Guide for Out-of-the-Money Call Premiums—*Now that you have rules to evaluate premiums for calls at the money, you can begin to evaluate similar out-of-the-money options (calls with a striking price above the stock price). First determine the premium if the stock price was exactly on the striking price. Then Rule 4 will show you how much to deduct when the stock price is at its current lower level.

Rule Number Four When the Striking Price Is More than the Price of the Stock—When the stock price is within a range of 90 to 100% of the striking price, the dollar value of the premium will fluctuate from its normal (Rule 1, 2 or 3) level by about 40 to

50% as much as the stock's dollar decline below the striking price.

To illustrate—when the stock price is 90% of a call's striking price, the call may have only 50% of its normal value. Should the stock price drop still further, the premium will continue to decline, but at a slower rate. Figure 5, page 115 shows how call premium values generally respond to changes in stock price.

You may use this curve as a guide to help evaluate initial premiums and also to indicate probable premium action should the underlying stock decline. In addition, it also illustrates the immensely favorable leverage, of perhaps 10 to 1 or more, inherent in calls that are slightly out of the money. They can be very profitable if the stock price increases.

In-the-Money Premiums—Two opposing forces are at work when the stock advances above a strike price. First, of course, there is the pressure of rapid build-up in the intrinsic value of the call. This tends to increase the premium point for point with any increase in stock price. However, a call entails more risk after its intrinsic value increases, because with any future decline in stock price its premium will now fall almost point for point—or about ten times faster than the stock, on a percentage basis.

The net effect of these two opposing forces is that the calculated time value reflected in the premium is somewhat reduced by the gain in intrinsic value. If the stock price continues to rise 20 or 30% above the striking price the call may sell for very little more than its intrinsic value. This relationship between option premium and stock price under extreme conditions is shown in Figure 7.

Rule Number Five for a Call That's Alive—If you are "in love" with a stock, buy calls far in the money when almost the entire premium represents intrinsic value. If you only "like" the stock, buy calls with lower premiums to minimize exposure to risk.

A call far in the money is not necessarily a bargain simply because its time value is near zero, even though it may have several months of remaining life. On the other hand, if time value is negligible, the call probably is a better buy than the common stock, especially if you intend ultimately to exercise it.

If you are attracted to an in-the-money call but do not intend to exercise it, there are many sound reasons to buy the one that has the least intrinsic value. It will provide greater leverage, less dollar risk and a lower investment.

Go Call!—Start the engine! Finally you are in the driver's seat with route maps and guides to help make profitable calls en route to your investment goals.

One final note of caution. If the market is stormy and the road ahead rough or slippery: slow down—pull off—await a more favorable investment climate before proceeding with your calls.

PART III

Selling Covered Calls

Calling in a Conservative-Defensive Direction

13 ═══════════════════════════════════════

Call on Calls to Bring Instant Income

Need more income? Then call on calls for your answer. No commuting, no boss, no office or factory—enjoy 24 hours of free time every day! You're not interested? Then why not tell your friends about it?

Option writing is pouring out millions of dollars of instant cash income every day to knowing early birds who have found the feeder. This bonanza comes from thousands of buyers of calls who gladly pay 2 to 3% of a stock's value each month just to have a brief call on it, as you discovered in earlier chapters.

This income is 20 to 35% annualized return on a seller's investment—far higher than the best rate of interest ever available to the public, and two or three times the 8 to 9% long-term total return (dividends and appreciation) which historically has been provided by all common stocks.

A 36% return is probably a maximum under favorable conditions, but even a realistic average total return of 25% is an attractive goal for the average investor.

Option writers (sellers), unlike buyers, need at least a modest portfolio of stocks or equivalent cash to get started. Capital requirements vary with the broker but writers generally consider $10,000 to $25,000 a minimum investment—the average is much higher.

You need not be wealthy, but as an option writer with a conservative-defensive approach, you must own at least 100 shares of the underlying stock for each call you write. This fully protects you against loss should there be an increase in the call premium. You are protected because whenever the option premium goes up, the stock should always have an equal or greater increase. By the time the call's expiration date approaches, its premium will have lost virtually all of its time value and reflect only intrinsic worth. Meantime, the option writer automatically has captured the same or a greater number of these dollars through the increase in market price of the underlying stock.

Premiums for At-the-Money Calls—If you write a call when your stock is selling at the call's striking price, the entire premium is time value. For example, in Figure 3, Kennecott Copper stock closed at $35 per share. On the same day the April $35 calls closed at 2½. The entire premium received was for the time value because intrinsic value was zero. The time-value portion of any premium, together with any dividends, is the writer's basic profit.

Premiums for In-the-Money Calls—So far we have been considering only calls written when the stock price and the striking price were identical.

In a bull market it is more common for a call to be in the money with part of its premium representing intrinsic value. This factor, you will remember, is the difference between the underlying stock price and a lower call striking price.

When you sell an in-the-money call, you should not consider the intrinsic value portion of the premium as profit. Rather, it is part of your cost. For an example, consider AT&T April 50's with a premium of 1⅞ when the stock was selling at 50⅝. A $50 call would have ⅝ intrinsic value, so the time value would be only 1¼.

Let's assume that you wrote such a call and supported it with AT&T stock which you owned, then worth 50⅝, or that you simultaneously bought stock at that price to protect the call. If this option is ever exercised, or if you ultimately buy it back, the transaction would be on the basis of its $50 striking price—not the 50⅝ market price your stock was already worth when you sold the call.

This point may seem unnecessarily complicated, but it is important to understand. Otherwise you would be liable to overstate your return-on-investment percentages, such as those shown in Figure 3, and perhaps sell calls for too low a premium.

Premiums for Out-of-the-Money Calls—What premium

Examples of Expected Annualized Rate of Return on Investment

			Expiration Months					
			April		July		Oct.	
Stock & Option	Striking Price	Stock Price Close Mar. 5	Premium Price	Expected Annual Rate of Return	Premium Price	Expected Annual Rate of Return	Premium Price	Expected Annual Rate of Return
AT&T	50	50⅝	1⅞	21%	2¾	12%	3½	9%
East. Kodak	90	90⅝	5⅛	42	8¼	25	10½	19
Ford Motor	35	35⅜	1 13/16	49	3¾	35	4⅜	24
Gen. Elect.	45	44	2	48	4¼	32	5⅛	22
Int. Harv.	25	25⅝	1 7/16	40	2¾	25	3	16
Kennecott C	35	35	2½	57	4	35	5	25
Kresge (SS)	25	24⅜	1⅜	57	2⅝	37	3⅝	28
MMM	55	55	3¼	50	5¾	31	8	26
Pennzoil	20	19	1	67	1 13/16	36	2⅝	29
Weyerhaeuser	35	34½	1 11/16	49	3⅛	29	4⅜	24

Figure 3 *Approximate annual rate of return on an option writer's investment that could have been expected from selling selected CBOE calls March 5, 1975, considering only those which were at or near their striking price.*

should be expected when you sell an out-of-the-money call? Obviously its intrinsic value is negative. Later, should the stock price advance to the striking price, any negative intrinsic value would be wiped out and the gain would go to you, the stockholder-writer. This means that the writer's normal profit from premium and dividends is sometimes increased by a stock price advance that wipes out this negative intrinsic value. Of course, there is no assurance that any stock will advance to its call's striking price. What happens to these premiums through common practice is that the market, in effect, divides this potential gain about 50–50 between buyer and seller. This is accomplished by subtracting about one-half of the negative intrinsic value from the normal at-the-money premium. This formula is valid, however, only down from the striking price by 5 or 10%.

This rule of thumb is demonstrated by a GE call in Figure 3. The April 45 call closed at 2 when GE stock was at $44. On the previous day GE closed exactly at the $45 striking price, and the call closed at 2½. This means that when the stock fell from $45 to $44, and the call's intrinsic value fell from zero to minus one, the premium fell by only ½ point.

Within a few days GE stock returned to $45 and the call premium promptly advanced to 2½. The buyer and seller each regained their half of the one-point increase. The one-half point gain for the option owner is obvious, but the writer's one-half point may be harder to identify. It is comprised of one full point by which the price of his GE stock increased, less the one-half point premium increase of the short call.

Examples of Option-Writing Profit Rates—Figure 3 illustrates several actual examples of option premiums and the annual rate of return each produced for a writer. These are randomly chosen examples of premiums *vs* stock prices on a single day.

In these illustrations, 50% of negative intrinsic value was added to actual out-of-the-money premiums, to indicate total return if the stock reached or exceeded the striking price. This seems reasonable, since in no example was the stock price far below the striking price.

Stocks may not always reach a call's striking price, and when that happens the writer does not realize this gain in the appreciation of his underlying stock. However, when the call is exercised the writer recovers all of the negative intrinsic value. The assumption that a writer should have an average gain equal to half of the negative intrinsic value on calls slightly out of the money seems reasonable because it probably happens even more often.

The examples in Figure 3 include only calls that were at or near the striking prices. Some were selected slightly above and others a little below, to illustrate patterns of premium changes under different typical conditions. These were early March transactions, which means that April call life was about 1½ months, July, 4½ months, and October, 7½ months.

As mentioned previously, actual income from in-the-money calls was determined by subtracting intrinsic value from the call premium and income for out-of-the-money calls was based on adding 50% of negative intrinsic value to the actual call premium.

Other adjustments could have been made but were not. They are relatively minor and would tend to make an overly complicated situation even more confusing. Then, too, some factors tend to offset each other. Even when we ignore them, the expected rates of return are understated, with the possible exception of very short-term calls.

Specifically, in Figure 3 no adjustment has been made for brokers' commissions paid or for dividends received on stock held. A continuous program of writing short-term calls would involve payment of a great many commissions. For this type of option-writing program, Figure 3 slightly overstates rate of return, primarily because there are so many commission variables that cannot be factored into a general rule. Commission expense on identical calls can vary as much as 300%, for example, depending on the quantity sold in a single transaction.

If necessary, however, the actual net annualized rate of return for short-term calls can be calculated separately for each transaction. To do this, include the cost of commissions paid and any income expected from dividends; then just use this simple arithmetic:

Annualized Rate of Return	=	(Adjusted (Call (Premium	+ Dividends − Commissions)))	× Turnover

Turnover = 250 divided by the number of trading days in the option's life. Adjusted call premium is the actual premium modified for in- or out-of-the-money calls as described previously. The number 250 is the approximate number of security trading days in a year.

There is a third adjustment that can be made, but it has not been factored into Figure 3 data. It is the reduction in seller's investment because the option premium is received immediately. This is a significant factor on long-term calls since premium dollars are larger and are retained longer. Reducing investment dollars by the 10% premium actually increases yield by about the same amount. For example, the Kennecott October call required an actual investment of only $3,000, rather than $3,500, because the call produced an immediate $500. If this 15% adjustment were made in Figure 3 the indicated annual return would increase 4 points, from 25% to nearly 29%.

When to Write Calls—You may sell calls spasmodically whenever you want or need instant income, or write them more or less continuously on a planned basis. If option-writing income is not needed for current living expenses, it may be left with your broker. After a few call premiums have been received, you can reinvest them in additional stock on which still more calls may be written.

Reinvestment of option income is a good defensive strategy for another reason. When you unexpectedly discover that you are in the midst of a bear market, reinvested option income helps soften the impact of any decline in market value of your underlying stocks. However, a discussion of this feature would lead us into option writing as a form of insurance on underlying stocks, the subject of Chapter 15.

Selling calls for instant income is just one reason you may find option writing profitable. The following chapters open the door to three other profit-making benefits, and Chapter 17 will provide guidelines to help you select and sell calls in a manner that should help you capture them.

But first, let's look at the second reason to sell calls—that is, to buy your favorite stock at a lower price, or unload your out-of-favor stock higher.

14

Buy Low—Sell High

Would you like to buy NYSE stocks at a discount? Most investors would, but unfortunately, individuals receive no discounts or premiums on stock transactions. However, you can, in effect, beat the system. The trick is to buy stock and at the same time write a call on it. Although an option premium is not regarded as a discount, it can provide similar benefits.

Money you receive from the sale of an option can be applied to reduce the amount you need to purchase the underlying stock. You need to supply your broker with only enough cash to make up the difference between the cost of the stock purchased and the premium received for writing the call.

The Kennecott example in Chapter 13 illustrated how a $500 option premium reduced the amount of money needed to buy 100 shares of stock from its market value of $3,500 to only $3,000.

If you prefer, you may view this $500 premium in the opposite way—as an advance payment, with $3,500 more to follow on an above-market $4,000 selling price, when and if the call is exercised. If the call is not exercised the $500 deposit will be surrendered to you.

Recognize your specific motives as you write each call. Anticipate the manner in which you expect it to be terminated. What happens at the end of the option's life can make a big difference in your tax situation. Also, when you plan that far ahead, terminal considerations may help to influence your choice of a stock to buy and an appropriate option to write.

For example, you may want to write a call which is likely to approach its termination date in the money. Then before it is called away, you should have decided in advance whether or not you wish to wait for the exercise, or buy back the call and keep your stock. Repurchase may cost more than you received when you wrote the call. Don't worry! Your stock will have gained more dollars than you lost on the premium, with a possible tax advantage. So regardless of how the call terminates, you have, in effect, either bought stock at a discount or provisionally sold it at a price which represents a substantial premium above the market price at that time.

Write Options in a Margin Account—When your stocks are held in a margin account, the option premium can be applied to buy more stock, or can be taken in cash. Under present margin rules this additional income could support purchase of stock worth double the amount of the premium. Specifically, in the Kennecott example you currently would need $1,750 plus commission to buy 100 shares at $35 on margin. But, by selling a call for $500 at the same time, the premium would cover $1,000 of the purchase price and you would need only $1,250 in cash to buy $3,500 worth of stock. The remaining $1,750 could be borrowed from your broker.

If you wish to continue to own stock after its price advances, and the call premium has increased as it nears expiration, do not overlook the need you will have for additional cash to repurchase the call. On the other hand, if the stock price is below the striking price when the call expires, you need do nothing. The stock will be yours, purchased at a "discount" with no strings attached.

Choosing the Stock and Option—The strategy of buying stocks at a discount, in effect, assumes that you will select one with which you are familiar and have a desire to own. After you have decided on the stock, you will choose an option from among several striking prices and expiration dates. These decisions will be easier to make and more likely to succeed if you will ask yourself two questions:

· Do I hope that the option will expire out of the money, so that I avoid facing the decision to buy or not to buy it back?
· Would I prefer to receive a larger immediate cash "discount" on the stock, with the knowledge that this strategy is

more likely to cause me to buy back the option at a higher price before its expiration date, if I still wish to keep the stock?

Before answering these questions, you should know that there may be tax advantages when you pay more to repurchase calls than you received at the time you sold them. This premium loss is also a tax loss, but at the same time, you will have stored a correspondingly larger tax-sheltered capital gain in the underlying stock. If you do not sell the stock in the same year it will not be currently taxable. When you do sell it later, profit may be taxed as a long-term capital gain at about one-half the rate of a short-term income-tax deduction that you took on the premium loss.

If you answered "yes" to the first question, you would probably want to sell an out-of-the-money call with near-term or midi-term expiration. When calls are very far out of the money, however, premiums often are so small as to be hardly worth writing. If this is the situation at the time you wish to buy your stock, you may decide to compromise and sell a call with a lower striking price or a longer life, or choose a different stock.

If your answer to the second question was "yes," you would write a longer-term option, probably one with a striking price near or slightly below the current stock price. This should offer the greatest dollar amount of time value, or discount, on your stock purchase.

Under any of these arrangements, you would only have a net loss if the stock price fell by more than the amount you received for writing the call. If it appears that this might happen, and you do not care to hold the stock for a possible recovery, it could be sold. However, you may not wish to do this because it would leave you in a net short position. The other possibility, when the underlying stock price has fallen several points, is to buy back the call for considerably less than you received for it originally. When it becomes unlikely the call will be exercised and so will ultimately expire worthless, you would only terminate it with a repurchase if you wished to sell the stock and not have a short call position.

Selling calls to buy your favorite stock at a discount is a conservative-defensive strategy, as is all option writing in Part

III. This definitely reduces risk in comparison with the purchase of stock where no call is written—although it also limits immediate opportunities for any potentially large capital gains.

You should, of course, determine in advance the maximum profit you can expect from sale of a call. When you know this, and the possible tax benefits, you are in a position to make an unemotional decision in your best personal interest. Then, if that specific proposition seems unattractive, look at other stocks or wait until the relationship between your stock's price and option premiums is more favorable.

Selling Your Stocks at a "Premium"—Selling stock at a premium above its current market price is another interesting strategy. After becoming familiar with the concept of buying stock at a discount, you will recognize this as merely the other side of the same coin.

This situation is one where you definitely want to dispose of a stock sooner or later, but sell at a good "above market" price, which you can negotiate right now.

The starting point in your choice of an option is a recognition that the lower the striking price, the more surely it will be exercised and the stock called. However, when an option is too far in the money, it has very little time value. It is vital to recognize this point because time value is the only quality possessed by an option that will enable you to sell the stock for more than its current NYSE market price. A call's current intrinsic value is of no advantage to you in this situation. The same dollars can be captured merely by selling the stock now.

The greatest amount of profit usually will be obtained if the call you write has a striking price just below the price you project for the underlying stock on the option's expiration date.

Lower striking-price calls will provide additional immediate cash and they are more certain to be called. However, if the stock is called, the total amount received will be less because you would have been paid fewer premium dollars for time value.

Statistics indicate that only a relatively small percentage of all calls written are exercised to purchase stock. This may cause you to wonder whether or not a call you sold would be exercised, even if it were about to expire in the money. No problem! It will be. In the very unlikely event that your call is not exercised, however, your gain would be even greater. In addition to the premium which you had already received, you would be free to sell the stock on the NYSE for more than you would have received had your call been exercised. Another alternative would be to write an additional call.

Calls about to expire, even with only a modest intrinsic value, will nearly always be exercised by someone. Floor traders for member firms of the NYSE can do this when intrinsic value is extremely small, because, as members, they can exercise the option and resell the stock with little or no commission expense.

Whether you view the proceeds of option writing as a discount when you purchase an underlying stock or as a premium when you sell, is important only if it helps you match your personal investment situation and your feelings, needs or desires with available opportunities in option markets.

In a similar vein, Chapter 15 will show how option writing can function much as casualty insurance on your stock might if a policy of this kind were available, which, of course, it is not.

15

Buy Option-Equity Insurance: Receive the Premium and Protection

Wouldn't it be great if when you bought a stock it came with an insurance policy which automatically protected you against declines in market value? Don't call Aetna or Travelers—they can't sell you this policy. Lloyds of London might insure your stock, but it would hardly be worth the time and expense required.

Protection of this kind is available—a fact which most investors don't realize because it is not called insurance.

There are several methods to obtain equity protection, but exchange-traded options are probably the best for most situations. OTC options also can be used in a variety of ways to protect against partial or total loss of a stock's market value. Along with these two types of options, there are a few other means to protect security values against decline. First, let's examine these other methods. Then we will be in a better position to understand the benefits of selling exchange-traded options as a protective strategy.

Why Protect Your Equity Values?—Every investor would like protection against loss. Most would be willing to pay a reasonable price for equity insurance if it were available. The mad scramble out of equities into Treasury bills, certificates of deposit and commercial paper at the first sign of a potential bear market dramatizes this great fear of capital loss characteristic of both individual and institutional investors.

Lacking protection against a bear market, this fear creates a stampede for exits, and too frequently it costs the entire economy hundreds of billions of dollars in abnormally depressed security prices. In just two years, 1973 and 1974, this cataclysmic loss of equity values probably cost investors more than the United States will pay OPEC (Organization of Petroleum Exporting Countries) nations for oil during the entire next decade.

Even had the Arab leaders been our security insurers, they could not have honored claims for the $500 billion or more of market losses sustained by U.S. investors during 1973 and 1974. A relatively small percentage of all outstanding stock actually changed hands during this period, but it seems that when only a comparatively few investors panic, their fear becomes contagious and the entire economy and equity market suffer.

What a difference it could make if even a few more of these nervous investors, including institutions, utilized optional means of protecting their investments instead of withdrawing from equity markets. Wouldn't it help to avoid or minimize these deep bear-market drops and provide more stability for the entire economy? And, if you happened to be among that small nervous group, might not you benefit most of all?

Convertible Protection—Most investors are familiar with some of these quasi-insurance-type investments. Best known are convertible securities, debentures and preferred stocks. These are popular because it is generally assumed that there is a minimum investment value and price beneath which the security will not fall. In better times it should have an appreciation characteristic similar to that of a common stock.

Protection afforded by a convertible is not always precise, but it can be substantial. The supporting floor is determined largely by the amount of its dollar income from interest or dividends. This gives it a minimum price level, not lower than the market value of a similar new nonconvertible investment which provides the same current yield. For example, the market price of a $1,000 convertible debenture with a 7½% rate of interest is not likely to fall below that of a similar quality nonconvertible security which yields the same $75 annually.

All convertibles are hybrids—a cross between a bond and a common stock. Each security seems to have its own characteristic price pattern and a chameleonlike quality when its common stock fluctuates in a price range where the conversion privilege is significant. As the value of a convertible increases, with an advance in the common stock price above the conversion ratio, or, in option terms, as the convertible goes further in the money, the degree of protection declines sharply. Protection offered by a convertible, therefore, varies over a wide range. It depends on the price action of the common stock, terms of the conversion privilege, and changes in national interest rates.

To place this in perspective, we might compare protection afforded by a newly issued convertible with that of a $250 deductible auto collision-insurance policy. But after a convertible's common stock price has increased substantially, its actual protection declines and it is more similar to a $1,000 deductible policy—or even just a common stock.

The real cost of equity protection via purchase of a convertible security may not be obvious. If you think of your purchase as a bond with an equity "kicker," this cost is the excess over the price you would pay for a similar nonconvertible security with the same rate of return. On the other hand, if your objective is to buy common stock with insurance, your cost should be thought of as the additional dollars you pay for the convertible over the current market value of the equivalent number of common shares for which the convertible may be exchanged.

Although the degree of protection may be little or great, and is subject to change without much notice, convertible insurance generally is long term, in some cases extending beyond the expected life of the investor. All other protective methods basically are short term.

Shorts Against the Box—Another method of protecting against a market decline is to "short against the box." This is accomplished by selling stock you own but do not plan to deliver until later. It is a short sale, but by maintaining ownership of the stock certificate you are neither short nor long—merely in a neutral equity position. The expression "against the box" describes this neutrality and implies that your certificate is being held by you, or for you by your broker, in a safe-deposit box.

When you no longer feel a need for this downside protection you can close out the short position by selling the stock you or your broker holds in the box, or you can buy and deliver additional stock.

A "short against the box" protects against loss, other than

two NYSE commissions, from the time you sell short until you cover. However, this takes you out of the market entirely, because you eliminate all possibility of any gain if there is an increase in the market value of your underlying stock. Shorts, in short, offer no advantage over closing out the position entirely, except that selling short can postpone the capital-gain tax you might have to pay if you sold the stock.

This review of limitations inherent in the two best-known protective measures should help us understand and appreciate the use of options for equity protection, as we now examine both the OTC and exchange-traded types.

Put Protection—Exchange-traded puts (explained in Chapter 21) have now joined OTC puts and straddles as the most thorough form of equity "price" insurance. Option protection for common stocks should now become much more popular, because trading OTC options had its limitations, and until recently these options were the only type available. The basic protection is the same for either type.

A put is exactly the opposite of a call. It gives a buyer the privilege of selling a specific stock to the writer at the striking price whenever he chooses to put it to him. Purchase of a put is the only certain method to protect against unlimited decline in a stock's market value without forfeiting any gains should the underlying stock price increase. It offers perfect downside protection with no loss of upside gains. Unlike a short against the box, a put does not forfeit your opportunity to participate in all price advances made by your stock. There are only two reasons why all investors do not buy puts for all their stocks. One is their inherently limited life—the other is cost. Although most puts are priced reasonably, considering their unlimited protection against a potentially dangerous risk, most investors have not availed themselves of put protection. Instead, when frightened, they either withdraw from the market or stay in and worry along on a sort of "self-insured" basis.

Put insurance, on the average, costs about ½% per week of the striking price. This compares with the historical total return on common stock investments of 8 to 9% annually, or about 1/6% per week. Put protection, therefore, costs about three times as much as the average long-term return on investment. This differential may not discourage occasional use of put protection, but it is obviously too great for investors to use with all stocks continuously.

When you intend to hold stock in a potentially risky climate, test the feasibility of put insurance by comparing its cost with the amount of fluctuation in stock price you might have to accept on a "self-insured" basis. If it appears that the put premium is less, it may offer an economical form of protection.

A put does, however, create instant built-in loss, equal to the put premium. A six-month put costs about 10 to 12% of the market price of the stock. Obviously, "self-insurance" will have cost less, if the stock does not decline by more than the amount of the put premium. Then too, until and unless the stock price also rises more than 10 to 12% during the life of the put, there is no net gain. The premium will have to be written off, at least mentally, against an increase in stock price before the put has any advantage over simply selling the stock and withdrawing from the market.

The combined "no-gain" areas, 10% below and 10% above the striking price, create a total "no-gain" band width equal to nearly 20% of the stock price. This suggests that put protection can be rather expensive unless you expect wide fluctuations in the stock's price, both up and down.

More could be written about the advantages and disadvantages of put insurance. Our primary purpose in looking at puts and non-option alternatives is to help us better understand the subtle protective characteristics of CBOE and AMEX call writing, when we look at that subject in the following pages.

Straddle Protection—Before investigating exchange-traded calls as equity protection, however, one other form of option protection should be examined. This one pays off whether your stock goes up or down—the best of both worlds! There is no catch; you cannot possibly lose anything—except the premium and commissions. And you don't even need to own stock to protect "it" with a straddle!

A straddle is very simple—one call plus one put, both at the same striking price and expiration date. You would exercise the call after the stock rose above the striking price and the put if it fell below. You might, with a little luck, be able to exercise both sides at different times, but don't count on it.

The only disadvantage of straddle protection is cost. Its price is the sum of the cost of a put and a call. For a six-month straddle you would expect to pay about 20 to 25% of the striking price. You would, without question, be protected for six months against any decrease in the stock's price and you also would benefit fully from any price increase. With a 20% straddle premium to absorb, however, the band of no profit widens to ± 20%. This means that the stock might move up and down a total of 40% before you even began to recover the cost of straddle insurance; so this may create a loss greater than that against which such insurance is supposed to protect you.

Call-Writing Protection—Chapter 13 considered the premiums received from the sale of calls to be additional income. Then Chapter 14 viewed them as a means to buy stock at a discount. Regardless of which strategy you select, there is, of course, only one premium. Now let's view this "buy stock–sell a call" strategy from another angle—equity protection.

Your first surprise must be that this form of "insurance" does not require you to pay a premium—you receive one! While you do not secure unlimited protection, since the maximum coverage is limited to the dollars received from writing the call, isn't it great to have an insurer pay the premium to you for a change!

Six-month premiums for calls at the stock's market price are a little more than 10%, so that has to be the extent of your insured coverage. It may not seem significant—but wait a minute. Those first few percentage points of price change must occur before points 15 or 20% below the current price are reached. Therefore, protection near the current price is far more valuable and desirable point for point of stock price change, than is protection far away from the market, such as that obtained by purchasing convertibles, going short, or buying straddles.

To illustrate such a seemingly rash assertion, compare this protection with collision insurance at various levels of deductible exclusions. For a car valued at $2,500, the $50 deductible insurance may cost four times as much as a policy with a $250 exclusion. The difference in dollars protected is only 8% but the added cost may be 400%, because the risk is so much more likely to become an actual loss between $50 and $250 than it is above $250. The even higher cost of zero deductible would provide a still more dramatic example of the value of protecting the first 10% of risk exposure.

Option writing as a form of insurance on equities seems, by comparison with auto collision protection, a very low-cost way to protect against those losses which have the highest degree of probability. On the other hand, the cost of protection against the relatively less probable risks of price deterioration offered by convertibles, shorts, puts and straddles looks quite high.

Since it seems clear that a worthwhile degree of equity protection can be obtained by selling calls against stock, let's look at specific ways to accomplish this and then give further consideration to overall advantages and limitations.

Our starting point must be that an optionable stock is to be protected—one which you now view favorably and would like to own. You plan to buy it and would if you had a protective cushion behind your purchase. Some form of stock insurance would be desirable because the timing of your purchase may prove not to have been at a favorable time, the entire market turned down or you just overestimated the company's immediate prospects.

To illustrate, let's return to the familiar Kennecott example. You may recall that 100 shares were purchased for $3,500 and a call was sold immediately. Its $500 premium was the protective cushion, a form of insurance which insulated the investor from loss even though the stock price might fall to $30 per share.

It's just that simple! You might think that the price of equity protection would be prohibitive, so it almost seems incredible that you pay not one cent for it. You do, of course, forego the opportunity to make an unlimited capital gain during the life of the call—that is, any gain in excess of that which is provided by the call premium and dividend. In the Kennecott example it would limit you to only a 25% annual rate of return on investment, which isn't too bad!

Although call writing as a form of insurance does not give you something for nothing, the defensive-minded investor will find this ceiling on profit a rather small sacrifice to make for the protection received. It is almost a case of having your cake and eating it too! If the stock price goes down, you do not lose until it drops by more than the call premium. If the price drops not at all or advances, you still enjoy a reasonable amount of assured profit.

To maximize protection, you would sell a call with a striking price very near that of your stock's cost, and one with the longest life. If slightly less protection is acceptable, you might sell a miditerm call instead.

When the call is terminated, either by repurchase or its expiration out of the money, you can write another call. In this way you maintain a protective blanket over your stock almost indefinitely.

More individuals and institutions are discovering the merits of option writing to protect their equity portfolios and increase income. This means that the supply of calls is almost certain to increase faster than demand. Competitive selling pressures are likely to bring reduced premiums—so don't wait!

This strategy is just great for the conservative-defensive-minded investor. Will it work for the more impatient speculative types, those investors who attempt to meet the problem of equity protection by putting out a few shorts when they encounter rough markets?

Strange as it may seem, an aggressive-defensive strategy for these investors also can be accomplished with less risk and expense through option writing, as we shall see in Chapter 16, in which we suggest ways to "Make Calls to Avoid the Short Trip."

16

Make Calls to Avoid the Short Trip

Can options be used to protect stock against sharper declines than the plan offered in Chapter 15? They can, but the technique is a little different.

You may recall that shorts against the box offer this protection, but that they were bypassed rather quickly because they offer no possible appreciation or income and have a built-in loss— specifically, two NYSE commissions.

One way to protect against sharp declines with options is to write calls far in the money and receive very large premiums.

Not all stocks with an exchange-traded option have calls available which are suitable for this strategy. There must be several different striking prices with most of them in the money. This is the only way that premiums can be obtained great enough to protect a large percentage of the stock's present value.

Figure 4 shows stocks which, on a single day, had calls at four or more striking prices, at least three of them in the money. To simplify the listing only the shortest-term calls are shown. Longer-term options with their still higher premiums and protection were, of course, also available.

For optimum protection you would sell a call at a striking price as low as you believe the common stock could possibly fall during the life of the call, or lower. This will yield a high premium and provide all the protection you expect to need. If the stock does not fall this far, or increases in value, you would buy back the call.

In summary, here is how this could work out:

· If the stock price falls as you expect it to, you consider the premium gain as an offset against the drop in stock value.

· If the stock price advances, you can repurchase your call at a tax-deductible loss. This would be more than offset by a greater increase in the value of your underlying stock. In addition to protecting stock against an anticipated decline that did not occur, a small net gain from the option's expired time value should at least cover part of the commission expense.

No option writing strategy will protect against a decline all the way down to zero, as a short against the box would do. You can, however, increase your protection to some extent by writing successive calls at lower striking prices if the stock declines to new lows. This involves multiple calls which, along with hedges and spreads, are reserved for discussion in Part IV.

It is interesting and worthwhile to understand why there are calls at several different striking prices on some stocks but not on others. This is because the exchange establishes new calls when, and only when, the underlying stock's closing price is at or near a new higher or lower price level corresponding to the next step in their standardized striking-price structure.

Incidentally, you can tell at a glance what the recent price history of an underlying stock has been, simply by referring to the daily table of option-trading data. You know that the stock recently has had a good price run-up if nearly all its options are in the money. On the other hand, you can be sure the stock has been in a sharp downtrend during the past few months if there are several striking prices and the stock currently is selling near the option with the lowest one.

Figure 4, for example, makes it quite obvious that IBM had a sharp rise from the 160's to around 220. The 160 or 180 calls would have protected against a rather sharp decline if either option had been sold at those premiums. Notice that these calls were so far in the money that there was virtually no time value remaining to provide a little profit, as well as added protection, should the stock decline and the call be repurchased.

Upjohn is the other extreme. Obviously it had been in a bear

Comparison of Various In-the-Money Call Prices

Stock	Call Striking Price	Call Premium	Stock Price	Stock	Call Striking Price	Call Premium	Stock Price
Avon	$ 35	4¼	$ 38⅛	McDon	$ 40	5⅜	$ 44⅜
	30	8⅛			35	9½	
	25	13			30	14¼	
	20	18			25	19⅜	
E. Kod.	100	2¼	92	Monsan.	60	1⅛	55¼
	90	6¼			50	5⅝	
	80	13¼			45	10	
	70	22¾			40	14⅝	
	60	32¼					
Gen. Elec.	45	4⅜	48⅞	Sears	80	⅛	67⅝
	40	8⅝			70	2⅜	
	35	13¼			60	8	
	30	16			50	17⅜	
					45	22¼	
IBM	220	10½	219½	Tex Ins	90	6⅝	92¾
	200	23⅞			80	13¾	
	180	40¾			70	23	
	160	60			60	33	
Kerr McG	75	1¾	67⅛	Upjohn	65	1/16	35¾
	65	6			50	3/16	
	55	13			45	½	
	50	17			40	1¼	
					35	3⅛	
					30	6¾	
MMM	65	1	56	Xerox	100	½	78
	55	3½			90	1⅜	
	50	6⅞			80	4⅛	
	45	11¼			70	10¼	
					60	18⅛	
					50	27½	

Figure 4 *Closing short-term call prices on a single day, for stocks with four or more call striking prices, most of them in the money.*

market of its own, since there were only two sets of calls with striking prices below the $35¾ stock price and there were several above. The sale of an April 30 call would provide stock protection only down to about $30 per share. Should Upjohn's price go lower, there currently was no option to provide further protection.

This illustrates one limitation of option writing as a means of securing deep protection. When a stock price remains near the bottom of its range following a sharp decline, no large premiums are available. However, after a stock has made a good recovery from a fall, this option-writing strategy can protect against a fairly deep price reaction, as illustrated by the IBM example.

One final note regarding protective option writing vis-à-vis a short against the box—you keep all dividends on the stock. With a short against the box, dividends are lost because a similar dividend is automatically charged against the short position.

Each of the last four chapters looked at one of the main reasons you might want to write options as part of an overall investment strategy. The basic approach was similar in each case, regardless of the specific reason for writing. However, to select one option for selling from among all those available may require additional explanation. Chapter 17 concludes Part III and looks at option writing as a single process which can be employed to enjoy one or all of these attractive benefits.

17

Complete Your Call—with No Hang-up

No need to agonize over the question of whether or not to sell a call—these decisions are really quite simple. First, do you presently own an optionable stock? If so, under what conditions would you sell a call? What if you do not own such a stock? We will also look at the circumstances that might lead you to purchase stock and simultaneously sell a call.

You probably own an optionable stock. Do any of the following statements reflect your present attitude? If so, consider selling a call; if not, you can forget it!

 · You want to keep your stock, but are concerned about a possible near-term decline in its market value.
 · You plan to keep the stock, but would like to have more income than provided by current dividends.
 · You would like to sell your stock in the near future for more than its present market value.

Now, let's assume that you do not own a specific stock with options available, but you are thinking about buying it. If any of the following statements express your current feelings, consider buying the stock and writing the call. But if none of these statements is representative of your current interests—buy the stock, if you wish, and forget the call.

 · You would like to buy the stock at a net cost which is below its present market price, either because you are a good bargain hunter or are concerned that the price might decline soon after you make your purchase.

· You would like to buy a stock that has made a comeback after being deeply depressed, provided you could do so conservatively by selling an out-of-the-money call as insurance.

Option Writing—a Way to Share Risk and Reward—While you think about your personal situation and weigh the factors that might affect an option decision, consider what actually happens to the risk-reward relationship when you sell a call.

The owner of any publicly traded stock accepts an unknown amount of potential risk and reward each day. A stock's total risk or reward will not change in the slightest degree tomorrow if you sell a call against it today. What does happen is that you share a portion of your potential risks and rewards with some stranger who purchases the call. Also, the seller's remaining risks and rewards are much more readily quantified than those assumed by the purchaser. The basis for your option-selling decision can be examined quite precisely in advance and should, therefore, be relatively less difficult to make than a decision to buy a call.

To put this statement in the most simple and homey way possible: the seller accepts two birds in the hand (the option premium and dividends) and gives up one in the bush (potential stock appreciation), receiving risk insurance as a bonus.

How to Decide When the Price Is Right—Assume that one reason for selling calls fits, so you are nearly ready to become an option writer. Your remaining questions should be: When? And for how much?

Large institutional investors put their option-writing programs on a computer. Each day they study a new printout that tells them the most attractive opportunities for selling calls, based on their own criteria. Most individual investors make their decisions without benefit of sophisticated equipment and generally act at random times when they happen to be attracted to a specific situation for any one of a thousand possible reasons.

This suggests that, rather than attempt to offer rules for timing your option writing, a more pragmatic approach would be to point out occasions when you probably should *not* act on these stray impulses acquired from various sources.

Obviously, whenever the potential for appreciation that you would give up is worth more to you than the reduction in risk, and increased income, you should not write a call. But sometimes even a trivial factor, such as a slightly higher premium, may change the balance in a more favorable direction for you, the seller. So, as with most transactions, the decision usually hinges on price. Therefore, before you begin to set your selling prices, wouldn't it be a good idea to know something about your costs?

As a prospective option writer, think of yourself as being in the business of manufacturing and selling options. The manager of this business certainly needs to know how gross income breaks down into expense and profit.

You can sell a few calls at a price that you believe represents "all the market will bear," but to stay in the option-writing business and make a steady profit, you should have a reasonable understanding of what it costs to support the calls you sell.

With option-writing experience you will acquire an instinctive feeling about the relative attractiveness of various call premiums. Meanwhile, to help you start in this business profitably, let's look at an example.

Assume that a $100 stock has a 6-month call with a striking price of $100 offered at a premium of 10, or $1,000. Would this be attractive to you?

Let's examine your costs. Investment would be $9,000 ($10,000 less $1,000 premium). The cost of money varies, but today a convenient nominal figure for individuals is about 1% per month. This charge is part of your cost structure, whether you borrow the money or use your own capital. Then, sooner or later, there will be two commissions on the stock and either one or two on the call, totalling a little over $200. If the stock pays a dividend, perhaps equal to 5% of its market price, or $500 annually, your transaction should be credited with dividends for one-half year, or $250. The entire transaction might look something like this:

Statement of Income

Revenues:
Sale of call	$1,000	
Dividends received	250	
Total	$1,250	$1,250

Costs and Expenses:
Cost of capital (@ 1%/month)	$ 450	
Commission expense	200	
Total	$ 650	650

Entrepreneurial Income
Before Taxes	$ 600*

_____

* Equivalent to $100 monthly or $1,200 per year, a 13% annualized return on assets after allowing for a capital charge of 12%.

It was relatively easy to sort out a few attractive opportunities for option writing when CBOE was new and calls were available on only 30 stocks. Today, with so many options to choose from on three exchanges, decision-making is more difficult.

The writer, faced with so many variables, needs to establish at least one constant factor of his own—a planned minimum return on assets utilized. By establishing the lowest acceptable gross profit, and then translating this into simple arithmetic, an experienced writer can almost instantly bypass the unattractive situations and sharpen his timing and profitability on transactions that merit a definite interest.

We have already assumed that the cost of money, even for comparatively safe investments, is about 12% annually, or 1% per month. The higher degree of risk assumed and the service provided by a writer is surely worth an equal amount, or another 1% per month. Added to this 2% per month total, there is commission expense for buying and selling the stock and its options. This cost will always be more than $100, or 1 point, for even the lowest-price stock and its calls. It will average 2 points or more for higher-priced stocks and option transactions.

When all these costs are considered, you will find that any time you buy a stock and sell a call for income, there should be a minimum premium of 2% per month plus about 2 points for commissions. For in-the-money calls, you would add an amount equal to intrinsic value. For calls out of the money by no more than 5 to 10%, deduct one-half of the dollar difference between the stock price and the call's striking price.

Even though a premium meets this minimum test, you should not automatically write the call. Testing the premium against your cost standards is only a filter or screen to quickly eliminate those calls that you would be quite unlikely to find rewarding.

Of course, you may relax minimum standards if your reason for writing is not income but protection—disposition of a presently held stock or the planned acquisition of a new one. Even in these situations, however, it is useful to test the premium offered against your rule of thumb at least to caution yourself against selling calls that are grossly underpriced in the market.

You can test the above suggested standard, or your own rule of thumb, against yesterday's option prices listed in *The Wall Street Journal, The New York Times,* or any paper that carries this data. For example, yesterday's papers reported closing prices of some midi-term calls with a life of four months. Let's examine those that were nearly right on the money. In the case of 4-month calls the rule suggests that the minimum premium should be 8% plus 1 to 2 points for commissions.

Avon $35's were one point in the money and sold for 5⅛. Eight times $35 is $280, or about 2¾ points. Commissions would add 1¾, making a total of 4½. Then add 1 point for the call being in the money, making the total minimum premium 5½. The call was trading at 5⅛, so our rule would say that you should probably reject it, or enter a limit order at 5½.

Kodak $90's, ⅜ out of the money, sold for 7⅜. Since 8% of $90 is figured as 7¼ points, this premium is only of marginal interest even if the stock were already in your portfolio. The same conclusion would apply to Exxon 70's. They were 1 point in the money with a premium of 5⅞. Ignoring commissions, this would hardly be of interest, even if the call were not in the money, since 8% of $70 is 5⅝. A premium of 8¾ would just about meet our minimum requirements. Perhaps at that price it was a call that should have been bought, not sold.

Homestake, selling at $45½, had calls at $45 which were reasonably attractive. Eight times $45 is about 3½. Then 1¾ points for commissions and ½ for intrinsic value adds up to 5¾, which was exactly the premium at which the calls were trading.

McDonalds, at $41½, had $40 calls selling for 6⅛. This was just a little below our minimum, since 8% of $40 is about 3¼, plus 1¾ for commissions is 5, and 1½ points for intrinsic value brings the total premium to 6½. This is a borderline situation and you might go either way.

This mental filter of arithmetic works quite well, although occasionally it may need to be adjusted. For example:

 · You want stock ownership with protection more than you need income.

 · As option writing becomes increasingly popular, especially among large institutions, some will cut the price and accept premiums lower than you can afford to take. If you want to write *those same calls,* you will have to meet their competition.

 · When stock market, economic climate or interest rates change rapidly, you may have to adjust your minimum formula.

An even simpler variation of this rule for minimum premium values can be used to help select the best option life to sell. Since there is a span of exactly three months between expiration periods, the 2% per month rule tells us that the next longer call should have a 6% higher premium. For example, when a stock and its call striking price are $50, there would be a 3-point spread between any call and the 3-month earlier one.

In actual practice, however, this price spread often is no more than 1% per month. When you face this situation, your decision whether or not to write a longer-term call will have to be based on other considerations, such as possible long-term capital-gain tax opportunities and lower annual transaction turnover costs, rather than merely the rate of return on assets.

The basic advantages of writing short-term calls vis-à-vis long-term calls are:

 · A higher per-month premium.

 · A shorter period of commitment, which means:

Less time your capital is locked up, and

Less possibility of market surprises.

· Additional calls can be written sooner.

· The premium reaches a zero time value and can be closed out sooner at a profit.

· Out-of-the-money calls are less likely ever to be exercised.

But long-term calls have their basic writing advantages too:

· They provide a higher dollar premium which:

Protects against a greater drop in stock price, and and

Gives the writer the use of additional premium dollars during the longer call life.

· Saves on commissions—up to 50%.

· Long-term capital gains are possible.

· Generally provides more dividends.

Graphical Analysis of Call Premiums—Many investors find that charts or graphs provide an easily understood "motion picture" of stock action. For others, these merely add confusion. Successful option writing does not require you to understand graphical presentations, but the explanations which follow should be useful if you are accustomed to think in these terms.

In Figure 5 the upward-slanting line represents the typical prices of 3- to 6-month calls at stock prices above and below the striking price. The curve is based on an assumption that when the stock is at the call's striking price the premium would be 10%. This is the point on the graph where the diagonal line crosses the vertical.

With the stock selling for 10% more than the call's striking price (a 1.10 ratio of market to stock price), the typical premium would be about 17%. For example, assume that a $100 stock has a $100 call with a premium of 10 when the stock and striking prices are both at $100. When the price of the stock advances to $110 the call premium should increase to about 17. On the other hand, should the stock price fall 10% to a ratio of .90, the premium would probably drop to around 5.

RATIO OF PREMIUM TO STRIKING PRICE
3- to 6-Month Calls

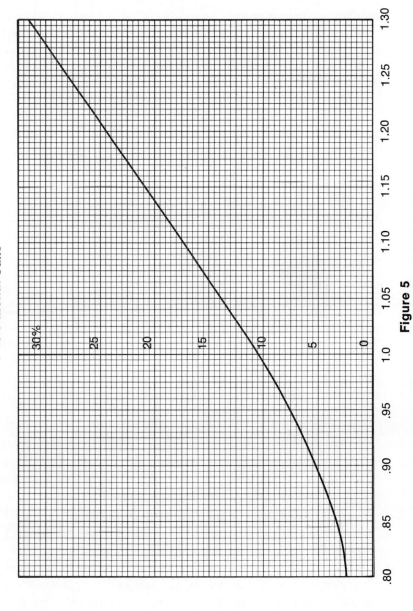

Figure 5

Ratio of Stock Price to Call Striking Price

Understand that this curve represents a more-or-less nominal relationship, does not consider Beta Factor, and is not necessarily consistent with previously expressed goals for option writers. In most cases the actual premium will be above or below the line. Any major discrepancy, however, can be very useful to you, because it may lead to an interesting application of the curve. Put in dots to represent the recent relationship between option premiums on a specific stock vs the ratio of market to striking price. When the points fall well above this curve, the calls may represent an attractive income situation for writers. If, on the other hand, the points fall well below the line, the call may be relatively underpriced. This should suggest caution to writers—a possible bargain for option purchasers.

This curve is based on drawing a more-or-less median line through a scatter-dot array of typical premiums for randomly selected CBOE calls.

Variations in a call's premium with changes in stock prices for situations where the call is far out of the money are illustrated in Figure 6. This is a rather unconventional way to use semi-log or ratio scales, but it shows that premiums on out-of-the-money calls drop at a much faster rate than the stock price.

Figure 7 represents the normal relationship between changes in stock prices and premiums for in-the-money calls. The straight line is the intrinsic value of the call. The slightly curved line just above is the nominal call premium. The space between them represents time value, which becomes smaller as the stock price continues to rise above the striking price.

These two charts also may be used to help suggest whether a call's premium makes it more attractive for purchase or for writing. This would, of course, depend on how far the call's premium fell below or above the nominal premium line.

To Buy or Not to Buy—That Is the Question; Or Is It?—In Part II you read of the many benefits to be enjoyed through purchase of calls. Part III has emphasized the advantages of selling them. At this point it may seem that you must choose which fraternity to join—the buyers or the sellers. Not so! Most experienced option traders are prepared to go either way, as may appear most profitable in the changing circumstances and opportunities presented by the markets each day.

**Approximate Relationship Between Market Price of a Stock and
A Distant Call's Premium When The Stock Is Below the Call's Striking Price**

Percent
Of Call's
Premium
At Striking
Price

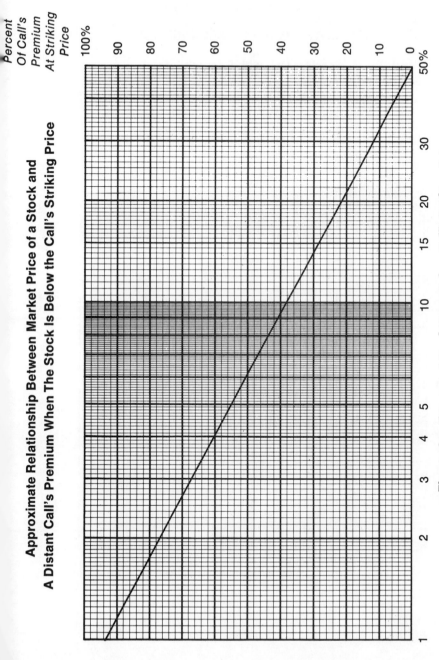

Figure 6. *Percent of Stock Price Below Call's Striking Price*

APPROXIMATE RELATIONSHIP BETWEEN
A STOCK'S PRICE AND
AN IN-THE-MONEY CALL PREMIUM

(Basis a Call with 6-Month Life)

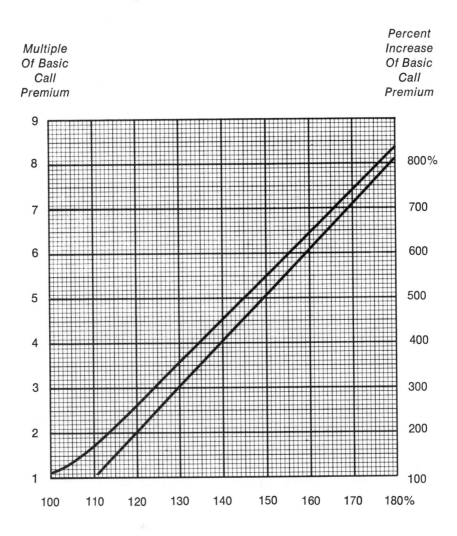

Figure 7. *Ratio: Stock Market Price to Call's Striking Price*

Should this attitude seem a bit inconsistent, prepare your mind for Part IV, which comes next. Here you will find advantages in selling and buying calls on the same stock simultaneously! These positions are called spreads, and are a form of investment hedging.

Hedging is an old practice which involves a wide variety of securities. In this book, however, we are interested in hedging with options, so let's move on to Part IV and see what hedge opt'ing is all about.

PART IV

Hedge Opt'ing

The Option Shock Absorber

18

Look Behind the Hedge for an Edge

Any investor who reads stock market and economic predictions in the financial press and investment-service publications should know what a hedge is. A sentence starting with the word "while," "since," or "although" is often the beginning of a hedge, and "however" frequently connects two legs of a hedged statement. Like this: "Prospects are bright for a sharp earnings recovery at the Hot Shot Electric, Inc.; however, new competitive pressure may force price concessions which cannot be offset by greater volume."

To hedge, whether in a simple statement or a security position, certainly is no crime. It merely signifies that the hedger has certain beliefs or bias coupled with a desire not to be damaged, should unforeseen circumstances prove him mistaken. The term "hedge" is very descriptive of its use in the security world. It was derived from the ancient concept of surrounding one's estate with a barrier, such as a hedge, to protect against unanticipated harmful circumstances.

Hedges—Old and New—Exchange-traded options are the newest, the most flexible and in many ways the most interesting investment to use for security hedges. However, we will first examine some older, more conventional types. This should help us to understand better the benefits and mechanics of these new option hedges.

Arbitrage, hedge and spread—These three sometimes are thought of as synonymous, but each has a distinctive meaning. If they are not familiar, you may refer to their definitions in the Appendix Glossary.

Arbitrage usually takes place in temporary special situations, so we can forget about it with respect to option hedges, although a call sold on CBOE against a NYSE-traded stock probably meets the technical definition of arbitrage.

Opportunities for hedges, on the other hand, are plentiful in every type of market: security, option and commodity. A hedge consists of a simultaneous short and long position on the same or a similar security. It is basically a defensive or conservative strategy with a surprisingly great amount of leverage.

A "short against the box" and an OTC straddle are examples of a complete hedge. The former is purely defensive and offers no opportunity for gain, while the latter is prohibitively expensive for most investors. The hedges we will want to examine are designed to make a modest profit with low risk and a small capital lock-up. They are created in the expectation that time will change this price spread favorably for the hedger.

We might start our examination of hedges by using a familiar old friend, option writing. This actually is a hedge, although historically it has not been referred to in this way. One reason is that until recently the only calls available were OTC options. These could not be coupled with stock into a viable hedge because there was no resale market (exchange) where the call could be bought back to close out the position.

In the language of Part IV, we could say that option writing consists of an exchange-traded call sold short and the underlying stock held long. The objective of such a combination is to profit by the difference between the current stock price and the call's striking price, plus its premium.

Let's look at two examples. Assume you own Kennecott stock trading at $35 and you sell a call for $5. You have created a hedge to benefit from a sure 5-point spread (KN at $35 vs the $35 strike price plus the $5 premium), provided KN stock does not stay below $35. For an out-of-the-money example, consider Atlantic Richfield at $80, with a $90 call at a $5 premium. The maximum gain from this hedge would be $1,500−(90 − 80 + 5) × 100.

As a second step in understanding hedgemanship we might look at various ways in which a corporation's common stock can be coupled with its convertible preferreds or debentures—even warrants—to create a hedge.

This time we will use Tesoro Petroleum as the example. On a day when its common was 15½, the 5¼% convertible debentures of 1989 sold for $93 and the warrants closed at 7⅜. Assume an investor purchased 10 $1,000 debentures, convertible into 526.3 shares of common stock, for $9,300. These could be used to create a bearish hedge by the short sale of 500 shares of common stock for $7,750. Since the debentures can be converted into more than 500 shares of common at any time, the maximum risk is only $1,550 no matter how high the shorted stock price advances.

This hedger expects the stock price to fall during the life of the hedge. If so, the value of the debentures would also decrease, but by a much smaller amount than the common. The 500 shares of common could then be purchased to close out the short position at a profit, enough to offset any loss on the debentures and still make a profit.

Tesoro warrants could be used in a similar way for a more aggressive hedge. Each warrant represents a call on one share of common at $13.80 until August 1976, when it expires. For this hedge assume that the warrants were sold short and hedged by purchase of the same number of common shares. Notice how similar this is to option writing—only two major differences. The warrant had a longer life than a call, and was issued by the corporation, whereas a call is created by others.

A 100-share long position cost $1,550 and the warrants sold short produced $738, making the total cash lock-up and risk about $800 plus commissions.

As August 1976 approaches, the short warrants must be repurchased (covered) even though they may be far out of the money. Having no intrinsic value, they probably could be purchased for only pennies per share, unless there was a huge short position which tempted warrant owners to "squeeze" the shorts. This example brings out a difference between the short sale of a warrant and a call—one which is usually a minor consideration. A worthless call need not be repurchased, but the short side of a warrant must be.

The end result of this stock-warrant hedge was accurately bracketed in advance. In a way it was a bearish hedge because if the stock price fell, it would be profitable until the common dropped to a break-even point at about $8. It is quite remarkable that such a hedge could protect the stock during a fall of nearly 50% and still be profitable.

It was a hedge which had a bullish characteristic too. While the stock was at $13.80 or above, the maximum possible profit would hold constant at about $5.70 per share, no matter to what extent the price of the shorted warrants increased. The $5.70 was generated by the short sale of warrants ($7.38) less $1.70 paid for stock in excess of the warrant exercise price.

This hedge had a spread of 8⅜ points. If at another time the spread were 10 points, the stock's break-even point would be 10 and maximum gain would drop to $3.80, less commissions. With these specific securities, the break-even point will always equal the spread, and the maximum gain will equal the exercise price less the spread.

*The Newest Hedge—Calls—*These conventional Tesoro hedges were less complicated than most, but still far more difficult to understand and execute than a simple option hedge using two calls. However, these examples help to prepare us by starting with a general perspective of investment-hedging concepts before we tackle hedge opt'ing.

A hedged position, using two calls traded on a single exchange, has several advantages over a hedged combination of other types of securities, usually traded on two different exchanges. For example, Tesoro debentures are traded on the New York Bond Exchange, the common stock on the NYSE, warrants on AMEX plus options on CBOE.

Some advantages of hedges using exchange-traded options, compared with those using other types of securities are:

· A single order to open or terminate a hedge can be entered to assure that both sides are executed simultaneously. Therefore you know that the hedge will be at this differential, or neither side will be executed.
· There is no confusion about lining up unrounded and fractional exercise ratios of convertible securities or warrants, or of possible changes in a conversion ratio.
· Commission expense on options, compared with that of stocks, is much lower.
· Short calls about to expire out of the money need not

be bought back; short warrants must be, even though intrinsically worthless for conversion.

· There are perhaps about 1,000 times more possible combinations to choose from among the various options. (These will be explained in Chapter 19.)

· Many popular stocks can only be hedged with exchange-traded options since they have no convertibles or warrants suitable for the second leg of a hedge.

Convertible debentures and preferreds, along with warrants, may have advantages over option hedges under certain conditions.

· Hedge life usually can be longer than the 9-month maximum for options, sometimes very much longer.

· When the convertible security is long, it generally yields interest or dividends, but this may be largely offset because the short stock will be debited for dividends earned while it is short.

· There may be an opportunity for wider spreads between the long and short positions in certain situations.

· Commission expense for debentures is low, perhaps even lower than corresponding option commissions, but stock commissions are much higher.

Execution—There are many different types of option hedges and reasons for using them. These will be discussed in Chapter 19. Before sorting them out, however, we need to become familiar with the mechanics for creating, holding and terminating any type of option hedge.

The short sale of a near-term call with the simultaneous purchase of a longer-term call at the same strike price is probably the simplest way to start. You might sell a call that expires in four months at $4 and buy a corresponding seven-month call at $5. This would give you a time hedge with a 1-point spread.

You would instruct your broker to short July and buy October at a 1-point spread, for example. He would try to execute your order on this basis. He might create the hedge for you by selling the July at 4¼ and buying October at 5¼, or sell at 3⅞ and buy at 4⅞, but, in any event, the spread would be 1 point or less. If your broker couldn't buy and sell at a 1-point spread, he would not execute one side and expose you to the risk of having only a short or a long position, unless you so authorize. However, he might suggest that you increase the spread by ⅛ point or so—again, that decision would be yours to make.

Because your July short call will always be worth less than your October long call, the only net charge against your account would be the $100 spread plus commissions. Of course, you would need to have considerably more funds in your brokerage account. To meet minimum equity rules, $2,000 or more would be required.

This hedge must be terminated in July at the latest. Action of the underlying stock during the time you hold the spread will largely determine how you choose to effect the termination. When the short July call expires, or is terminated, you no longer have a hedge. In addition to having received the premium for selling a call which may have become worthless, you also own a long call with a 3-month life. Its net cost was $100 plus two option commissions.

If the July short call was worthless, the October call would not be in the money either; but if the stock was only slightly under the striking price, the call should be worth at least $2. Later it might be worth much more, since the stock may rise substantially during the remaining three months of call life. This call could then be terminated at a profit, just as any other option described in Part II.

If the July short call is in the money near its termination date, it can be repurchased for more or less than was originally received. In any event, July's time value would be nearly exhausted, while October's would not. October also could be terminated, probably at a small profit on the hedge, or held in anticipation of greater profit during the next three months.

In this chapter and its examples we were merely attempting to help you become acquainted with some general background information about the use of options for hedging. As we explore the subject further in Chapter 19, you will find option hedges can be attractive because:

· The premium received from the short sale greatly reduces the amount at risk on the purchase of a long call.

· When the long call is at a lower striking price or a more distant date than the short call, the spread between the two premiums (plus commissions) is the maximum that can be lost on a one-for-one hedge.

· A wide variety of hedge possibilities exists, because options are available with different striking prices and three expiration dates. Combinations may be selected to reflect the investor's personal bias or view regarding the probable pattern of stock movement over the next nine months.

· When the underlying stock price has moved significantly in either direction, the protective side may be removed by selling the long call or buying back the short one. This may help maximize profit, because to maintain a hedge beyond the time needed for protection may reduce potential gain on the protected side.

· Opportunities exist for favorable Federal income tax treatment of capital gains.

When your calls are all long, as in Part II, or short, as in Part III, you are on a one-way road, either up or down. This is just great, as long as you are pointed in the right direction. Hedges are a dual-lane highway where for a while you can go up and down simultaneously. This allows time for you to become acclimated to a new environment before deciding which direction is most to your liking—toward the summit or the valley. Chapter 19 is loaded with directions to hedge you either way.

19

Spread Your Calls to Hedge the Falls

Perhaps this chapter should be called "How to Win While Losing," or "How to Lose While Winning." The idea of hedging, of course, is to gain more than you lose, and, chances are, if you will take time to understand option spreads and what can be done with them, they will help you to become a steady winner.

The basic idea of option spreads is deceptively simple. You simultaneously buy and sell options that are nearly identical. This exposes you to only a relatively small risk, with many interesting ways to gain.

We will look at six different strategies in this chapter. Multiply this by nearly 200 stocks with exchange-traded calls at three time periods and one to six striking prices, and you have a lot of material available for building a hedge.

Investors experienced in both option and stock market trading learn to handle option hedges as a carpenter uses his kit of tools, to carve out an investment structure based on a pattern of anticipated movement in the stock price.

A good way to build your option hedge is to look six to nine months into the future and define your view of the overall market direction, with special emphasis on the price trend you anticipate in any underlying stock whose options you might consider using in a spread.

Each type of hedge has its own characteristics, yet its performance is flexible and subject to market changes. The challenge in hedge opt'ing is to choose an option which seems to fit your expectations for a certain stock's trend, and to match it with a suitable hedge in a manner that promises to maximize your profit opportunity and minimize risk.

Five major types of option spreads, plus the bearish call-stock hedge, will be examined in this chapter. You may find these identified elsewhere by other names, because option spreads are so new that nomenclature is still in a state of flux. In order of their appearance here, they are:

- Time Spreads (Horizontal or Calendar)
- Bullish Price Spreads (Vertical)
- Bearish Price Spreads (Vertical)
- Ratio Spreads
- Sandwich Spreads (Butterfly)
- Bearish Call–Stock Hedges

The Time Spread

This consists of the simultaneous short sale of a near-term call and purchase of a more distant one, both at the same striking price. Potential for gain derives from the fact that some time value remains in the more distant long call, after the short call has virtually none and is about to expire. Risk is minimized since both the long and short positions tend to move in the same direction with changes in the price of the underlying stock.

Figure 8 illustrates four different patterns of stock-price action that can occur after a time spread has been created on its options.

The first curve, "A," represents a stock-price pattern which is hard to predict but would generally result in the most attractive payoff. After the spread is established, the action, in theory, would be about like this: The stock would decline, finally going below the short call's striking price, so that the option will expire worthless. This would allow you to retain all of the short-sale premium as income. Then, during the next three months, the stock price recovers; the remaining long call, the second leg of the former spread, finishes in the money for a very attractive long-term capital gain. This hedge can be very profitable, but it is tricky. Try it with a stock you believe is likely to decline below a

EXAMPLES OF TIME SPREADS
(July Short and October Long)

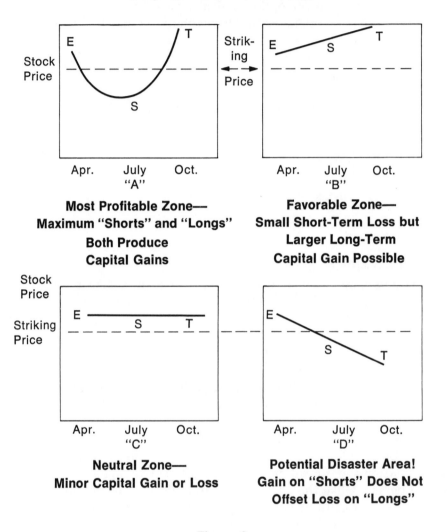

Figure 8

E = Execution of Spread
S = Short Expires
T = Long Terminates

striking price for a few months and then bounce back rapidly. If you are right, you can make a lot of money.

The second pattern, "B," represents a stock whose price advances during the entire life of the spread. Before it terminates, the short call must be repurchased at a loss. The spread could be closed out at any time, perhaps at a small profit. However, you will probably wish to retain the long position after the short has been closed out, unless the trend in the stock's price has become weak. Your greatest profit should come from holding the long call for three additional months. In any event, when the short leg terminates, the hedge has ended. The second leg should be held or sold on the same basis as any other long call under the same conditions.

The third pattern, "C," is that of a stock whose price remains flat—no substantial price increase or decrease during the life of the spread, and certainly none near the call's expiration date. With this stock trend the short could be repurchased at a profit, but the long call would have lost about as much as the short gained.

The one to be avoided under all conditions, of course, is "D." During the few weeks after the short leg is covered or expires worthless, it is very easy to believe that your underlying stock is following pattern "A" and not "D." This may be costly self-deception. If there is a possibility that the stock will continue in a declining trend, you should seriously consider the sale of your remaining long call while it still has some slight gain. This might at least help you to offset commission expense.

Early Termination—We have assumed, for the sake of simplicity, that all calls will be closed out or allowed to expire near the end of their lives. You may, of course, terminate either leg of a hedge at will. This can introduce interesting pattern variations in the basic spread strategies.

Let's see what happened when this was done in an actual use of a time spread. Eastman Kodak stock was selling for $132. A $140 January call was sold short for $650, and an April $140 call was purchased at $875 to form the hedge. The premium difference or spread was $225. The total risk was $225 plus commissions.

After the spread was created Kodak stock did not perform

well. It appeared that the price was unlikely to reach $140 by January, and that the entire $650 received from the short-sale premium, less $25 commission, would become profit. Then, if Kodak's price recovered to over $140 in the following three months, in accordance with pattern "A," the April call would acquire intrinsic value. For example, Kodak stock at $160 by the end of April would produce $2,000 additional profit on the $140 April long call.

Instead of following "A" and advancing or maintaining its price, however, Kodak continued its sharp type-"D" decline. Both call premiums dropped almost daily along with the common stock. The January call fell even faster than the April. It seemed clear that the anticipated stock up-trend would not occur. The January short position had done its job of hedging the long April call. The only reason to continue to hold the declining April call now was to protect the January short. But the stock was far below the striking price and had only a relatively small amount of life remaining in a depressed market. The short no longer appeared to need this protection.

The long call was sold for $625 only a month after it was purchased. Loss was $250 plus $50 commissions. The short call, which by then had declined to $237 from $650, continued to fall and ultimately expired worthless. Its gain was $650, less $25, a net gain on the spread of $325. The profit was equal to about 100% of the total amount which had been at risk. Of greater significance, however, is that this favorable result could occur in a market that completely reversed its trend in less than one month, invalidating the assumptions on which the hedge was established. The "A" anticipated pattern had become "D," yet, by simply selling the long side of the spread after it was of no further use, an almost certain loss was turned into a reasonable profit.

It is interesting to compare results of this option hedge with ownership of Kodak stock. During those two months, shareowners suffered paper losses of $2,500 per 100 shares—perhaps even more if they continued to own it.

You should consider, too, what might have happened to the short call if the trend again reversed after the protective long leg had been removed. Had the price gone up slowly and failed to reach $140 by the end of January—no problem. However, if it increased rapidly, it might have gone above $140 before expiring. In this event, if the stock price remained above $143, the hedge probably would have terminated in a loss.

Prescriptions for Time Spreads

Stocks to Use—Use a stock whose current price action is dormant or weak, yet one you are confident will move substantially higher, starting in a few months. If you know of a stock whose price pattern you can reasonably expect will follow Figure 8, pattern "A," you should enjoy substantial tax advantages and a high percentage of profit *vs* dollars at risk.

Striking Price to Use—Use a striking price which is near or slightly above the stock's current market price. Generally avoid calls that are very far in the money. One reason is that the short call is more likely to be exercised just when you would rather it wasn't.

Option Months to Use—Short the nearby or midi-month. Buy a similar call with a 3- or 6-month longer life. Actual choice of months will be determined by your feeling about the time that may be needed for the underlying stock to move up, and on the amount of premium spread between the two calls. If the difference between the midi- and distant month is less than 1% per month times the market price of the stock, the more distant call is probably the better buy, assuming it fits your plans.

Normal Premium Spread—This will depend on several factors; the volatility and popularity of the underlying stock, the relationship of striking price to current stock price, the remaining life in the short call, and the trading activity in the two calls. The range is from just under 1% to a maximum of about 2% per month times the market price of the stock.

Suggested Selection Procedure—Review the points of spread which have existed between the proposed short and long premiums during the past few weeks. When this difference seems to be at a minimum, enter an order for the spread based on this differential as a maximum, plus perhaps ¼ point at your broker's discretion, if needed. Should your broker persuade you to position only one side at a time, the spread may become greater than you expected, making it difficult for you to realize your planned profit goals, or even to avoid a loss. When a spread is created as a hedge, both sides should be completed simultaneously.

You can, of course, establish a delayed hedge to protect an existing long or short position. The actual points of spread would therefore be entirely dependent on the premium of the newly acquired position.

Bullish Price Spreads

This position consists of the simultaneous purchase and sale of similar calls with identical expiration dates but different striking prices, the short call's being higher. This is also called a vertical or perpendicular spread. It would be used when you believe that a stock price will increase to equal or exceed the higher striking price.

When any price spread has a substantial amount of life remaining, the difference in the two premiums will be less than the $5, $10 or $20 difference in their striking prices. In the price spread, this premium difference, plus commissions, represents your maximum risk, even though the stock may have fallen far below the bottom striking price when the spread expires.

Maximum profit will occur if the stock is on or above the higher striking price by the termination date. It will be equal to the full difference in striking prices, less the original spread cost and four option commissions. Unlike the time spread, this one does not have the remotest possibility for a greater gain.

The maximum gain or loss of a bullish price spread can be determined the instant it is established. However, potential profit is not very great under any conditions. The reward-to-risk ratio is only fair, with the spread established when the stock is at or above the lower striking price. When both striking prices are out of the money, however, reward-to-risk ratio is better, but, of course, the probability of total loss also is very much higher. Multiple and ratio spreads, discussed later, are more popular variations which contain greater opportunities for profit *and loss*.

Prescription for Bullish Price Spreads

Stocks to Use—Use a stock whose price is quite stable, although it probably will have to be one that has suffered a recent price decline in order for it to have two or more striking prices, at least one above the current price of the stock. Preferably choose a stock which sells for $50 or more so that the spread between striking prices will be $10 or $20, rather than $5 with lower priced stocks. This is suggested to minimize the effect of commission expense, which is quite a high percentage of maximum gain with this type of spread. The stock should, of course, be one you expect will advance during the life of the spread.

Striking Price and Months to Use—A single bullish price spread is not a particularly attractive option combination, since it is only based on an attempt to capture the small differential between the premiums of two calls versus the spread between their two striking prices. The month to use should be far enough into the future for the long position to advance near to or above the short's striking price, but it should not be so distant that the stock is liable to fall below both striking prices, causing the long position to expire worthless too.

Let's try an example. XYZ Company stock closed at $75. An April $75 call premium was $8¾ and the $10 higher striking-price call sold for $5. A bullish price spread would cost the difference between the two premiums, $375 plus about $100 in commissions. This would be your maximum risk. Figure 9 shows that if the stock closed at $85 or above four months later, the spread would yield maximum profit, a net of $525 ($1,000 less $475, including commissions). The spread break-even point would be with stock at 79¾ on the last day for trading April options. Between $80 and $85, profit would increase point for point with the common, as shown graphically in Figure 9. With stock under 79¾ the spread would terminate at a loss, reaching a maximum of $475 at a stock price of $75.

Bearish Price Spreads

This consists of one call sold short at a low striking price, hedged by the simultaneous purchase of another call at a higher striking price, but with the same expiration date. As the name suggests, it is designed for use only when the underlying stock is expected to decline.

It bears some resemblance to our Part III option-writing ap-

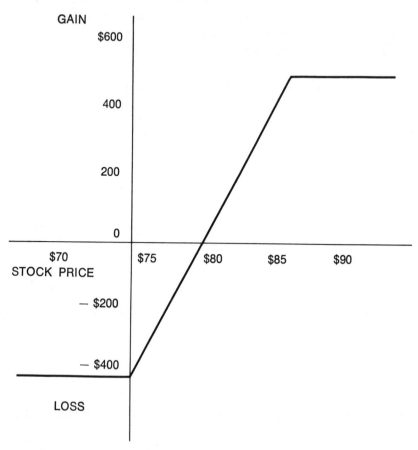

Figure 9. *Example of a Typical Bullish Price Spread*

proach, except that purchase of an out-of-the-money call is used as a hedge instead of the underlying stock. Results, however, are quite different. With option writing you make a profit regardless of how high the stock price advances. With a bearish price spread you tend to lose if the stock advances even the slightest amount after the hedge is established. Such a loss under the worst conditions, however, would be relatively small—limited to the difference between the two striking prices less the difference between premiums.

Profit is assured if the stock price declines as expected. It would be equal to the difference between the two premiums, less commissions. The bearish price hedge has two advantages over straight option writing. Much less capital lock-up is required. An even more important feature in a bear market is that the investor does not own stock whose value would surely drop point for point with the short. Risk is relatively small and limited, but it occurs when the stock price goes up—not down. By comparison, option writing is a hedge against minor declines in the stock's price. However, it is subject to increasing downside loss should the stock price fall beyond the amount of premium received. This is not true of the bearish price spread.

This spread is also a conservative alternative for anyone who might consider writing a naked call, the subject of our next chapter.

Bearish price spreads may seem less complicated if we use an example. Merck stock closed at $75 on a day when a four-month July $70 call could have been shorted at 9½ and the $80 call purchased for 4⅛, a difference of 5⅜.

What would have been the outcome? Maximum risk occurs if the stock is over $80 at the end of July. You then would lose $468 plus commissions. Maximum gain of $538 would be realized if the stock is below $70 at that time. Note that, whatever the gain, it is produced with very little capital lock-up.

In Figure 10 (A and B) potential profits and losses for this bearish price spread are compared with those which would result from writing an identical call against stock at the same time. This indicates that option writing is a bullish strategy while this spread is definitely bearish. So, despite their similarity, one is not a substitute for the other.

Note in Figure 10B that a $70 option written on Merck would have produced a $950 premium, but with the stock at $75 this offered a potential net gain of only $450, since the call was $500 in the money. Break-even points for the writing would be at stock prices of about $66 and $79. The upper break-even point is where option's intrinsic value would have exceeded the premium, and the lower point is where the premium would no longer offset the loss on stock purchased at 75.

The spread's break-even point was 75⅜. Profit would increase to $538 if the stock price fell to $70 or below. Above 75⅜

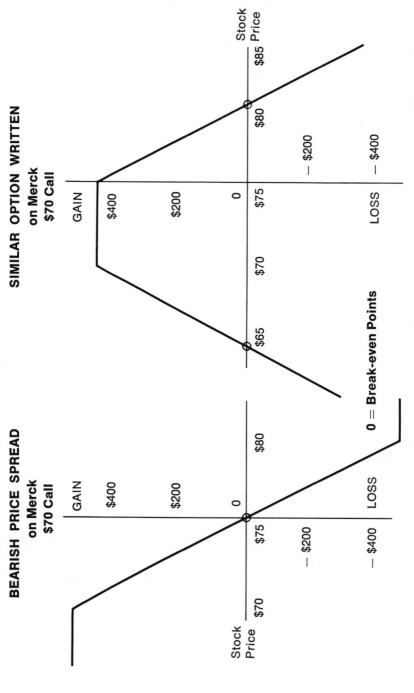

Figure 10A.   *Identical $70 Merck Calls:*   *10A hedged by an $80 Call*
10B hedged by stock purchased at $75.

Figure 10B.

BEARISH PRICE SPREAD on Merck $70 Call

GAIN
$400
$200
0
LOSS
—$200
—$400

Stock Price $70
$75
$80

SIMILAR OPTION WRITTEN on Merck $70 Call

GAIN
$400
$200
0
LOSS
—$200
—$400

$65
$70
$75
$80
$85

Stock Price

0 = Break-even Points

the spread would incur a loss, reaching a maximum of $468 at a stock price of $80 or above.

Prescriptions for Bearish Price Spreads

Stocks to Use—Use only those stocks which you believe will be weak performers during the next few months. Higher-priced stocks with $10 or $20 spreads between striking prices are generally to be preferred over those which have only $5 steps between striking prices. Use the same criteria you would employ in the choice of a stock for a short sale.

Striking Price and Month—When a stock has multiple striking-price calls, the lowest ones offer the greatest opportunities for profit, if the stock goes into its expected sharp decline. However, these also carry a greater risk should the stock surprise you and go up. Consider what could have been the result in the Merck example, had the $60 call been sold instead of the $70. Maximum profit would have been $1,238, rather than $538, if the stock fell to $60 or below by the time the call expired. But what if the stock price rose to $80 or above instead? Loss on the $60 call would have increased to $768, instead of $468.

The best expiration month is the earliest one that you believe will allow you to realize your planned optimum gain.

Ratio Spreads

This is merely a price spread with an unequal number of long and short calls. For example, you might have a price spread by selling three short calls and buying one long call at a lower striking price. This would be a 3:1 ratio spread. This is sometimes referred to as a "partial hedge" because, unlike ordinary price spreads, it is unbalanced in a way that leaves some calls unhedged and vulnerable to stock-price changes above their striking price.

Despite the added risk, this ratio spread has highly attractive characteristics, especially in a bear market. The short sale of several out-of-the-money calls produces a substantial premium income and usually pays for the premium on purchase of a similar call which is in the money. This income from several calls increases profit potential, lowers capital lock-up and greatly increases downside protection. With the stock above the striking price of the short calls, however, the risk increases rapidly.

Here is what happens. The stock price goes up and the long call acquires more intrinsic value. This value is at its maximum for the spread when the stock approaches the striking price of the multiple short calls. Beyond that point all gain evaporates rapidly as the stock continues to rise.

To clarify the characteristics of ratio spreads, let's look at an example using Texas Instruments. The stock was at $100 per share. A January $100 call traded at 6⅜ and the $120's at 2¼. The sale of three $120's would produce premium income of $675 while purchase of the $100 call would cost $638. The premiums are about in balance, although there is $37 credit to help on commission expense.

Nothing unusual happens as long as the stock price stays at $100 or below. Any advance in stock price between $100 and $120 causes the $100 call and the spread to gain value, about dollar for dollar with the stock-price increase. When the stock price crosses $120, however, the value of the spread will drop $2 for each $1 increase in stock price. This is because the $100 long call could only hedge one of the $120 shorts. The other two are naked, with no hedge to protect you as they acquire intrinsic value.

In this example the calls obviously had short lives, as indicated by the relatively small premium on the $100 call. However, the price of a stock like TXN can move up fast. If it did, the three short calls at $120 might cost more to buy back than could be realized from the sale of one $100 call.

Figure 11 shows terminal results of this example under stock prices from $100 to $140. It shows that you would have no money at risk as long as TXN was not above $130 when the spread expired. If you are a conservative investor, however, you probably would terminate this spread before losing the paper profit of about $2,000 when the stock was selling at $120. If the spread were maintained by a less conservative investor until TXN stock reached $150, the loss could be over $4,000.

A similar example using a lower-priced stock is shown in Figure 12. This chart would apply to any 3:1 spread on a stock in the $30 to $35 price range where one $30 long call was purchased

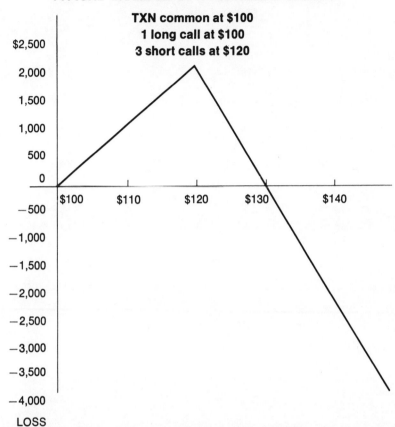

Figure 11. *Break-even point and maximum-gain point of a 3:1 ratio spread on Texas Instruments.*

and three $35 calls were sold short for an equal number of premium dollars. Notice how quickly the gain evaporates when only 5 points separates the two striking prices.

Bearish ratio spreads also could be created involving several short calls sold at a striking price *below* that of one long call. The only reason to create this arrangement would be to receive substantial premium income and then hope that the stock price did not go up the slightest amount before the shorts expired. This spread is seldom used because risk is very great and potential

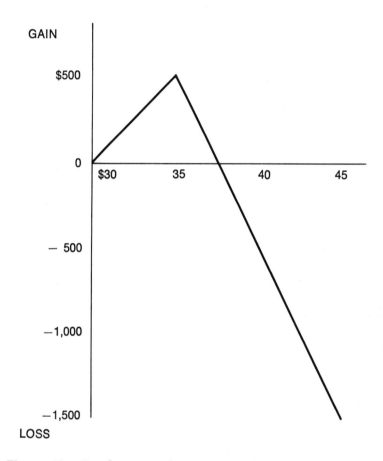

Figure 12. *Break-even and maximum-gain points for a lower-price stock. Gain or loss assumes a zero difference between premium received for 3 short sales and that paid for one long call.*

reward small. It is, in fact, hardly more than a group of naked calls with one small bikini for protection.

Prescription for Ratio Spreads

Stocks and Calls to Use—Use short-term calls with two striking prices preferably 10 or 20 points apart, both out of the money, or the lower one near the current stock price. The stock should be depressed enough so that it is not expected to go through the higher striking price, yet strong enough to approach it. The calls to be sold at the higher striking price should have a significant premium, generally ¼ to ⅓ that of the call to be purchased at a lower striking price.

Ratio of Short to Long Calls—Personal judgment is involved, but the following points should be considered before creating a ratio spread:

   · Premiums received for selling the short calls should generally total about the same as the dollars paid for the long call, plus commissions. This way you have no money at risk until the stock advances to near the point where the short calls are in the money.

   · If fewer shorts are sold, the premiums received may total less than that paid for the long call. This difference would increase the amount initially at risk. Fewer shorts, however, may create less ultimate risk if there is a possibility that they might terminate in the money.

   · When the stock price starts to approach the striking price of the shorted calls, you can be in for some rather unpleasant surprises. No advance signal rings to tell you the amount of time value or intrinsic value these short-call premiums might acquire. This is the reason the short leg usually should be covered before it reaches its striking price, unless you are very bearish about the near-term price of the stock and don't mind taking a loss if you are wrong.

   · Confine this spread to the earliest expiration date so it will have less than three months' life.

   · Select shorts with a striking price far enough out of the money to decrease the possibility that the stock might reach this point.

· Monitor your position regularly. Your short calls may never actually go in the money and may ultimately expire worthless, but their time value still can cause you sleepless nights if the stock price approaches the striking price.

· Do not attempt a ratio spread until you are comfortable doing 1:1 price hedges—perhaps not even then!

The Sandwich Spread

Yes, there really is such an option! It consists of four or more calls, identical except that they are at three different striking prices. One long call is at the high and one at the low striking price, and two short calls are at the midi-striking price sandwiched in between.

Prescription for Stocks and Calls to Use for a Sandwich Spread

The stock must have calls with at least three equidistant striking prices in the same expiration month, preferably not the most distant one. At least one, preferably two, of these must be out of the money. Premiums received from the two calls sold short should about equal that paid for the two long calls. Optimum profit will be achieved if the stock price falls right on the striking price of the short calls when they are about to expire.

Reward and Risk—Characteristics of a sandwich spread may be easier understood if we use an example, such as the Merck spread in Figure 13. This is based on the same price data we used earlier in the Merck bearish spread. Along with those July $80 calls selling for 4⅛ and the $70's at 9½, there were July $60's trading at 16½. With these three different striking prices we could construct the following sandwich spread:

Buy 1 $60 call at	$1,650
Buy 1 $80 call at	413
Total Cost	$2,063
Sell 2 $70 calls at $950 each	
Total Received	$1,900
Net cost, less commissions	$ 163
(Also is total amount at risk)	

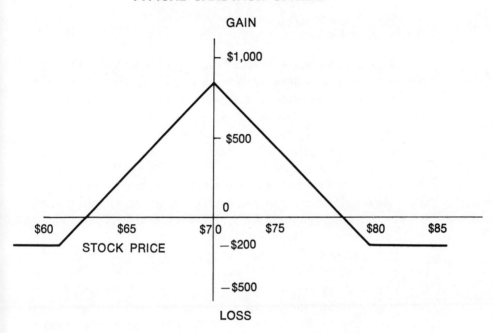

TYPICAL SANDWICH SPREAD

Figure 13. *Points of maximum gain and loss for a typical sandwich spread.*

This spread would break even with stock at 61⅝ at the bottom and $77 on the high side. As long as Merck stock was priced between these points when the calls expired, the spread would have profit. Maximum gain of $837, less commissions, would occur with stock at $70 on the expiration date.

Timing—There are just a few occasions when the sum of the two long-call premiums nearly equals or exceeds that of the two in-between shorts. If you can ever find these rare ingredients of a sandwich spread, and if they are to your taste, you should not hesitate to buy because within an hour the numbers may not be as favorable for you.

To have good fun and cheap entertainment, study daily CBOE and AMEX trading records and attempt to discover potential sandwich spreads with near-zero risk. It is good exercise in arithmetic even though you may never actually buy a sandwich spread for yourself.

Stock-Option Hedges

Options also can be used as one leg of a hedge with stocks and convertible securities. Option writing is a form of this hedge where stock is long and the call is short. In this chapter we will look at the reverse situation—stock short and the call long. But first, let's take a brief look at stock short sales.

Only a relatively small portion of all stock trades involve a short sale, and these are handled much differently than option short sales on their respective exchanges. When you buy stock there is no indication as to whether or not the seller sold it short. Every original option transaction, however, is a short sale, usually protected by ownership of another security.

If you wish to sell a stock short, you will arrange through a broker to borrow the stock from an owner, knowing that some day you must replace it. In most cases you will do this at some future date by purchasing stock, paying the market price at that time. You hope this will be lower than the price you received from your short sale, but it may be much higher.

Short sales of stock can be highly profitable in a bear market or a sharp downtrend of an individual stock. However, unless you are in close contact with the market, adverse price movements may occur before you can close out your position. Many short sellers have suffered severe financial losses because they maintained a short position too long when the stock price advanced.

Purchase of a call can provide outstanding protection for a short sale of stock. During the life of the call, it guarantees that the short can be covered at the call's striking price any time you wish to do so. The call protects you even if the market runs up strongly against the short because when the stock goes above the striking price, the intrinsic value of the call premium rises and thus offsets the deficit being accumulated by the shorted stock.

Purchase of a call to protect short stock does create a temporary built-in loss equal to the option premium and commissions. However, with several call striking prices available, you can select one that is out of the money. This provides less than maximum protection, but it costs less. If you prefer complete protection, choose one that is in the money with a striking price near where the stock was shorted.

When you sell a stock short, it would be with the expectation of receiving a large capital gain through a sharp drop in the stock's price. Purchase of a call to hedge the short generally requires a relatively small portion of the anticipated gain, and adds a great feeling of safety—not a common emotion among most short sellers!

Assuming the stock you choose to short has exchange-traded options, the only major consideration is time. No exchange-traded call has a life of more than nine months. If you plan to keep the short longer, a replacement call could be purchased as the original approaches expiration.

This hedge has so many possible variations, nearly each one different, that no attempt will be made to offer prescriptions. Also, it is quite simple to plan and execute, particularly by comparison with some of the option spreads we have encountered in this chapter. Now that so many of the most popular stocks have exchange-traded options, this hedge should become very popular in future bear markets.

Monitor Your Expectations—You are likely to enjoy more consistent success if, before attempting to execute any spread, you make a record of the favorable results you are anticipating. Also, make note of unfavorable situations that might possibly occur. Plan and record the steps you might take to terminate or modify the spread on a favorable basis, should a problem arise.

Benefits from this simple bit of informal planning will far outweigh the time required to do it. First, you should be more relaxed while holding the spread. Second, contingency plans can help avoid costly procrastination in a possible crisis so that you will be more decisive when decisions are required.

A third advantage is that a record of the spread results you anticipate will be available to compare with actual performance, and thus enable you to review your hedge transactions for ideas that might improve future profitability.

Three of the four major option strategies have been presented so far. The last, discussed in Chapter 20, is one not recommended for any but professional investors or traders who are in constant touch with the market. This option strategy is known as going naked—which means, selling short with no hedge, not even a bayberry leaf, for protection against the bulls.

No one will be offended if you skip Chapter 20 and go directly to 21. But if you are curious to know more about how "Going Naked Could Leave You Stripped"—read on.

PART V

Selling Naked Calls

20 ═══════════════════════════

Going Naked Could Leave You Stripped

You may believe that if you were to sell an option or stock you don't own, you could acquire the image of a nineteenth-century con artist who had sold the Brooklyn Bridge to an unsuspecting immigrant.

Borrowing and selling securities or options when you don't even own them is no crime. In a way, it's analogous to borrowing a cup of sugar from your neighbor. Of course a bull might borrow sugar when it was selling for 10 cents a pound, but he wouldn't go short. When the price reached 75 cents a pound, he would try to terminate the obligation by giving his neighbor a dime. On the other hand, a bear would borrow sugar with the price at 75 cents and expect to replace it in kind when the price fell back to 10 cents.

Although this is a chapter about option short sales, you may be more familiar with selling stock short than you are with naked calls. A comparison of differences and similarities between these two may help you better to understand the advantages and problems of selling uncovered options. Before your broker can execute a stock short sale for you, he must borrow the shares from an owner. This situation does not apply at all to options. As with commodity futures, one short option must exist for each outstanding long position. There cannot be more longs than shorts. By contrast with this inherent 100% short position in options, stocks sold short at any one time are never more than a fraction of 1% of all outstanding shares.

Most sellers of calls, however, are not naked. They hold a similar option or underlying stock as a hedge to protect against a sharp runup in the stock price and option premium, as we have seen in previous chapters. However, experienced sellers are sometimes so confident that the price of an underlying stock will drop that they are willing to sell naked calls and accept risk of potentially large loss. They would rather do this than hedge and thereby dilute potential short-sale profits. Dilution does take place, of course, when you hedge with a stock or option that declines in value while the short becomes more profitable.

Many dramatic episodes in Wall Street history involve personal tragedy associated with an overextended short position on stocks.

Short selling can be hazardous even in a bear market. In the late 1960's a number of professional security analysts started private hedge funds, based on attempting to capture profit from stock downtrends through short selling. Apparently most lost money, many closed, and few, if any, new ones have been created recently.

Since professional analysts and investors have difficulty making a profit selling stocks short in bear markets, what chance is there for an individual to sell naked options successfully? Before you answer, consider that a naked call has about 10 times greater risk than its underlying stock. While the dollar risk on a given 100 shares is about the same for the stock and option, the option investment is only about one-tenth as great—hence it involves ten times greater risk per dollar.

Were the potential dollar gain of a naked call also ten times greater than a short sale of the same stock, this might be an interesting gamble—but it isn't. If anything, the potential reward may be far less because your maximum potential gain is limited to a portion of the option premium, whereas when a stock is sold short, your gain is unlimited point for point as the stock declines.

As a further indication of the risks of option short selling, even among professionals, it has been rumored that the demise of a major national brokerage house in the late 1960's may have been hastened by a $1,000,000 loss from the sale of naked OTC calls.

To put it bluntly, selling naked calls is a hazardous high-risk low-reward pursuit, which should only be undertaken, if at all, by experienced traders, and carefully monitored with contingency plans for limiting loss.

Now that you have been cautioned and are no doubt pessimistic about dealing in naked calls, you should also be told that over the life of any single set of options, all buyers' net gains or losses must equal all sellers' net losses or gains, less commissions. In other words, if buyers overall have lost, short sellers have gained, whether they were hedged or naked. Sellers who hedged had part of their gains offset with losses on their long positions. This includes writers who lost, or failed to gain, on the value of their underlying stock. When short-sale profits are not diluted by offsetting losses, it is possible to make some very substantial gains.

Naked calls are not very popular, however, except for those which are far out of the money. Otherwise, the ratio of naked calls to all calls sold is probably comparable to the percentage of naked short sales of popular stocks as against their total sales. The low-premium, far-out-of-the-money short-term calls, which might be referred to as "casino calls," are purchased by speculators as an outright gamble—not as an investment.

With due recognition of inherent risks, it must be admitted that the sale of naked calls is one of four basic option strategies. If, after thoughtful study of a specific situation, you believe that the sale of naked calls would be an attractive strategy for you at a particular time, here are a few suggestions to help avoid being stripped by the bulls:

    · Be as certain as possible that there is a strong probability the call's underlying stock price will head down sharply over the immediate term—especially be alert to protect yourself if it moves up close to the striking price.

    · Deposit more than your broker's minimum initial cash or equivalent margin requirement to use in closing out the position if you are wrong.

    · Don't sell naked calls on more shares than you would be comfortable with if you were short the common stock. Calls far out of the money might be an exception on a limited basis.

· Determine in advance how much you are willing to lose, and make definite arrangements with your broker so you do not fail to buy back the calls before this point is passed.

· Monitor your position daily. Whenever the call premiums approach your close-out price, or when the stock is active and trading on an uptrend near this point, consider covering your shorts.

· Reduce your potential loss by lowering this close-out price as the call approaches its expiration date and has lost much of its time value.

· Uncovered calls in a ratio spread are just as dangerous as any other naked calls. However, as long as you recognize that they are unprotected, you may be inclined to watch the entire spread more carefully.

Despite all the technical and fundamental stock market signals and inputs used by sophisticated investors, it is generally agreed that no one can tell positively which way the price of a stock will move in the next few hours, days or months.

Unless the probability of a decline is overwhelmingly favorable, selling a naked call is hard to justify. If you firmly believe that a stock price just "must" go down, a better way to take advantage of the situation might be to sell the stock short and buy a protective call, as suggested in the previous chapter. Unless you feel certain that the short-sale gain on the stock will be so great that a call premium is very small by comparison, you probably should reconsider and question whether or not any form of short offers enough reward to justify the risk in that specific situation.

PART VI

Buying and Selling Puts

21

Bears Put—Bulls Do Too—Shouldn't You?

Exchange trading of puts, new in 1976,* was scheduled by CBOE, AMEX and the SEC for introduction three years after the exchange-traded calls began to be traded. This may tell us something. Doesn't it point up the advisability for new option traders also to allow time, perhaps as much as three years, to gain expertise in calls before moving on to puts?

Many readers may already have developed their skills in trading calls, and option newcomers may wish to know what lies ahead after they have mastered calls, so let's take a brief overview of this new form of option security.

Puts and Calls Compared—A put is similar to a call at the same striking price and expiration, with one exception. The put buyer has only a right (option) to sell the underlying stock to a put writer—not, as with a call, to buy it. In other words, the put buyer can take 100 shares of stock and put it to the seller, who must buy it at the striking price—perhaps far above its market price at the time of exercise.

You might think of a put as a mirror image of a call. For example, when stock is above the striking price, its put is out of the money; in the money when the stock price is below the striking price. You would buy a put only if you believed the price of its underlying stock was likely to go down. You would sell a put if you thought the stock price would advance, or at least not fall by as much as the put premium you received.

Ways to Use Put Options—Several approaches suggested for trading calls in Parts II and III can be reversed and modified for use with puts. To illustrate, in Part II, Buying Calls, we examined

* As this book was going to press, the Securities and Exchange Commission decided to delay exchange put-option trading until after January 1, 1977.

Route 1: The Alternative Way. The mirror image of this is selling puts against fixed-dollar investments. This is not always a current equity alternative to buying a call, but it would provide immediate extra income and the possibility, if the stock is put to you, of buying the underlying stock later at a "discount."

It would work about like this: If the put terminates with the stock price above the striking price, you keep the put premium as additional income and with very little commission cost. However, if the stock falls below the striking price, you have a choice—to repurchase it or wait for the stock to be put to you. If the stock is under the put's striking price by less than the premium, you have, in effect, bought the stock at a discount over the price you would have paid for it on the day you wrote the put. If, when the stock is put to you, its market price has fallen by a greater amount than your premium, you have a loss. But if your alternative to selling a put was to buy the stock, you have at least enjoyed a limited form of "insurance" equal to the premium received.

In general, you would sell puts when you have more confidence in a stock than seems evidenced by the market. Your objective would be to earn a substantial amount of immediate income at little commission expense or carrying charge, if you are correct, and minimize your losses if you are wrong.

In order to write puts you must keep cash or marketable securities in your brokerage account to cover purchase of the stock in the event the put is exercised. However, this is merely a standby situation, and no interest is charged. In fact, the put premium gives your account an immediate credit, which may reduce interest charges if you are in a debit position.

Now—what about buying puts? The basic strategies for selling calls in Part III can be accomplished many times through buying a put rather than selling a call. This is not to say that selling a call is the same thing as buying a put. In the first place it is obvious that when you sell a call you receive the premium, but when you buy a put you pay it. Selling a covered call should be considered a neutral-to-slightly-bullish tactic, while buying a put is definitely bearish.

Buying a put differs from selling a call in other ways. In Chapter 15 we saw how you can secure a form of limited "price" insurance on your stock by selling calls, and thereby receive—not pay—a premium. Puts also have an insurance characteristic. For this, however, you pay a premium, but instead of a 10% (more or less) insurance against a price decline, you receive unlimited downside protection for the life of your put.

The most common use of a put is as a direct substitute for the short sale of a stock. Buying a put can be more expensive than a stock short sale if the stock price goes up or down by less than the cost of buying a put. However, a put is a much safer speculation. If the stock goes up, potential losses on a short sale are unlimited and actually can become enormous. The maximum loss using a put as an alternative is limited to the premium cost.

Calls and puts frequently may be viewed as alternatives in a specific situation. Your decision will depend on how well the slightly different characteristics of each option match your current investment goals and strategies, and the relative attractiveness of their premiums.

Ways to Combine Puts with Calls—The introduction of exchange-traded puts as an alternative to and supplement to calls adds an important new dimension to the world of options. Of even longer-range significance, however, is the new possibility of combining exchange puts with calls into a single transaction. For example, a straddle is the simultaneous sale of one identical put and call. Now, with the introduction of marketable puts, an exchange straddle is possible.

Prior to the advent of exchange-traded options, straddles were very popular with OTC option writers. During the three years when only calls were available on option exchanges, the ratio spread became a sort of substitute for the straddle, the strip and strap (see Option Glossary). To illustrate: a trader would write two calls against only 100 shares of stock, leaving one naked. The larger premium would be comparable to that received from one OTC straddle, supported by 100 shares of the stock. In other words, a ratio spread starts out with a premium similar to that of an exchange put plus a call.

The end results from these two approaches, however, can be quite different. When you write a ratio spread and the stock price rises above the striking price of the naked call, you accumulate losses point for point without limit. The straddle writer under similar conditions is perfectly safe. He retains all of the put and call (straddle) premiums regardless of how much the stock price increases.

The ratio spread does have one important advantage over a corresponding straddle, if the stock price falls below the striking price. The ratio call writer has two "insurance" premiums to offset the loss in market value of his underlying stock. The straddle writer, however, faces two dilemmas. Not only has the value of his underlying stock fallen, but there also is the legal obligation to purchase 100 more shares at the striking price—well above the current market price.

Try to avoid either of these problems. Write a ratio spread only if you feel sure that the underlying stock price will not go up much, if at all, and write the straddle only if you believe the stock will not go down far.

Exchange-traded put and call spreads represent another interesting combination, and one which is more conservative than straddles. Here the put and call may be at different striking prices, for example, the call at 80 and the put at 70. As long as the stock price is within this 10-point range, there would be no exercise, and both premiums would be retained by the writer. For instance, if a total premium of $1,000 was received, the writer's "no loss" band would be 30 points wide, from 60 to 90. Naturally, a writer's premium and risk would both have been higher for a straddle at either striking price.

At first glance it may appear that the use of puts in these new exchange straddles and spreads gives results similar to the older vertical-call spreads, but they are actually quite different. For example, consider a vertical (price) spread where you would buy a 70 call and sell a similar 80 call. It is not necessary to own the underlying stock to establish this fully hedged position. Your maximum gain (at 80) is 10 points, less the premium difference and three or four commissions. Your maximum loss (with the stock at 70 or below) is the premium difference plus commissions, making the total "no loss" band about five points (more or less) between 70 and 80.

Using puts, the nearest equivalent to this approach might be to sell a new exchange-traded put-call spread at 70–80 and protect the 80 short call with stock. In this way you would retain the full premium (perhaps $1,000 to $1,500) as profit if the stock stays at 70 or above. The downside break-even point would be in the low 60's (70, less about one-half of the premium—the other half being considered as an offset against the drop in market value of your underlying stock). Writing this spread also provided "price" insurance for your stock, assuming that you would have held it whether or not you wrote the call.

Of course, the most exciting feature of exchange-traded puts, whether bought or sold separately or in combination with calls, is that they can be closed out quickly on a national auction market. Unlike OTC puts and straddles, where you had to wait for your profits and suffer with mistakes for as long as 6 months and 10 days, you can now eliminate any position on a reasonable basis and take your profit or cut your loss merely by making a phone call to your broker.

We learned at the start that buying a call is similar to renting a car. Continuing this analogy, the new role played by exchange-traded puts might be compared to renting a boat to trail along behind the car. Puts go along with calls, too, and they can take you to places you would find difficult to reach using only calls. But don't abandon the option road maps acquired earlier. Continue to use them with calls, and then adapt them to include puts for an even faster and safer trip.

Some readers may wish to stay right on terra firma with calls, but many investment goals are easier to reach when you include this second mode of option travel. So, after you have established your skill as a call operator, why not try your talent as a navigator of puts? They come in many sizes to fit bulls and bears alike.

Every option is a futures contract. CBOE dusted off the two centuries of cobwebs from the OTC-option structure and zoomed that versatile security into the twentieth century. Having read this far you probably will agree that these new exchange-traded options are a modern security and a tool capable of meeting an extremely wide variety of investor needs. But in this rapidly changing world, what of tomorrow? The final chapter considers this question and offers a few comments on "Your Future in Futures."

PART VII

Futures

22

Your Future in Futures

Future growth and popularity of stock futures, the functional description of options, seems assured. They offer many new ways to make and save money—methods impossible to duplicate by any other means. Among these are premium income to supplement dividends and a useful degree of protection against a future price decline. There are perhaps 15 or 20 of these unique benefits of exchange-traded options, detailed in the preceding chapters.

Certain of these option features will appeal to you more than they do to other investors. With all this variety of option benefits, there must be some that could be valuable to every active investor on certain occasions, when option applications are more widely understood. Increased trading activity, news stories and the advent of many new option advisory services are all indications that a great many investors have already discovered new ways to accomplish their personal goals more easily, and with greater safety, by the thoughtful use of option-trading techniques.

The future of these stock-futures markets seems assured, but what about your future in them? Option exchanges, like all public markets in a free economy, impose no barriers. No special educational or employment background is needed to enter and become rich, nor will impeccable credentials prevent you from losing a fortune. In other words, you will be on your own.

Two types of individuals have very little future in this business. The plunger who dives in and immediately loses probably will not, and should not, return. The speculator who has great initial luck is likely to pyramid his winnings until he, too, loses all and retires from the field.

Those investors who do have a future in futures will use moderation, limiting their maximum-risk exposure to losses which they can absorb without serious injury—then will make every effort to avoid even these.

Option trips are like flying a plane. Your greatest risks are at the point of takeoff and landing. With options there is no need to take a position in foul weather. When just learning to fly with calls, get a good flight instructor—a knowledgeable broker. Don't try to solo until you have a successful dual operating-experience record.

Start by writing a call on stock you now own but plan to sell soon in any event. This corresponds to acquiring initial flight experience in a Link Trainer—you still have both feet on the ground and can't possibly get hurt.

After you have enough experience to feel comfortable flying alone, just treat your option vehicle as a faster and safer way to reach certain investment destinations, to which you might otherwise travel by slower and perhaps more risky means. Integrate your options with other investments to maintain a powerful, balanced portfolio.

To survive in the world of options an astute investor should also be a reasonably active one. Extended lapses of interest or attention while at the controls can create serious problems. The capability of doing simple mental arithmetic, especially percentage calculations, is as useful to an option trader as navigational competence is to a solo flyer—and for about the same reasons.

Before you consider bringing options into your investment picture, one question you may want answered is: Do options fill a sound economic need, or are they merely the latest fad in speculative public games?

The answer to the first part of the question is, yes—they play a vital protective role, which is beginning to benefit the entire field of equity investment. Although only in its infancy now, this insurance function is slowly becoming recognized by individual and institutional investors.

Try to think of any commodity, merchandise or service produced in America that you cannot protect with insurance. Homes, including the validity of their titles, autos, health and medical care, savings accounts, even cash in your wallet—all can be insured against loss—nearly everything, that is, except the value of your equity investments.

The advent of exchange-traded options, instituted by CBOE in 1973, provided a means whereby the investing public could secure a form of equity protection more easily than they could insure their household goods. Because it is new, completely unfamiliar to most investors, and not called "insurance," relatively few of the 25,000,000 U.S. investors have availed themselves of this protection.

The need for massive amounts of price insurance on common stocks, however, was never greater or more dramatically illustrated than by the tragedy of the 1971–74 bear market, when an estimated $500,000,000,000 was lost by owners of U.S. common stocks.

The investing public gradually will learn to respect writing calls as a form of insurance that can protect the value of their common stocks in critical periods—perhaps at all times. Others will buy puts and calls as two different types of insurance, each guaranteeing that their maximum loss will not exceed the premium paid.

In the future, when the technique of using options to protect stock values becomes better understood, option exchanges may ultimately fulfill a role comparable to that of the insurance industry in its protection of life and property.

Exchange-traded options, long overdue, have at last arrived. You are a little late to become an authentic pioneer, but there is still time for you to stake out a claim to expertise before the field becomes overcrowded—before it becomes apparent that, for nearly all investors, "Futures Are in Your Future."

Epilogue

Your option profits or losses will always be related directly to the price performance of the underlying stock. With no firm conviction about the direction a stock's price is likely to take during the next few months, you probably should avoid both the stock and its options.

Bullish? If it is your belief that a stock is, or soon will be, in an immediate uptrend, and if you are right, there is no faster way to profit than to buy its calls. Also, remember that this form of equity participation is the only one that guarantees you a strict limit on potential dollar loss if you are wrong. Of course, don't forget, either, it is also the only one that offers no protection against a fast 100% loss. Even if you are right about a stock's price trend, it is important to buy only those calls that best match your overall investment plan. Chapters 6 through 12 help you do this succesfully.

Neutral? You may want to stay in the market even though unsure about its near-term trend. If so, there are several potentially profitable courses you might take, providing you are not downright pessimistic. When you currently own stock and want to keep it, write calls (Chapters 13 through 17) for greater income and protection. If you do not own a stock, you may buy it and write calls and/or puts (Chapter 21).

Bearish? When you believe that a stock's price is about to experience a substantial decline, you again have several choices. Write ratio call spreads (Chapters 18–19), naked calls (Chapter 20), or buy puts (Chapter 21), depending on the degree of your pessimism.

First—and Last: Even before you classify yourself currently as a bull or a bear, you should have decided whether you will use options defensively or aggressively, or in an intermediate position on the Chapter 2 option compass. Then later, if you measure your performance as an option trader, profits may or may not be sensational, but the real test should be whether or not put and call options have been used in sensible ways to help you travel faster or more safely in your chosen investment direction.

Option Glossary

AMEX   The American Stock Exchange

ARBITRAGE   The purchase of a security on one market and the almost simultaneous sale (which may be a short sale) of the same security in another market at a different price.

AT THE MONEY   An option is "at the money" when its striking price and the underlying stock price are the same.

BEARISH   The attitude of any person who believes that stock prices will decline.

BEAR MARKET   One in which the majority of stocks does decline substantially.

BETA FACTOR   A figure that represents the historical relationship of a stock's price volatility to that of the stock market as a whole. A Beta of 1.00 indicates normal movement. Zero would mean no price change at all, and 2.00 is the maximum for a stock with a history of wild price fluctuations.

BULLISH   A person who believes that stock prices will rise.

BULL MARKET   One in which the majority of stocks is rising substantially.

CALL   A contract, or limited form of security, which obligates the writer (seller) to deliver, upon demand of the buyer, 100 shares of a named stock at a specified price at any time during the life of the call.

CBOE   The Chicago Board Options Exchange, pioneer developer of marketable options.

CERTIFICATELESS TRADING   Marketable options are among the few types of security that do not at present evidence ownership by issuing a transferable certificate. A broker's confirmation is the only document necessary.

CLASS OF OPTIONS   Options covering the same underlying security.

CLOSING PURCHASE TRANSACTION   A transaction in which an investor who is obligated as the writer of an option intends to terminate his obligation by a closing purchase transaction of an option of the same series as the option previously written. This cancels the investor's

173

pre-existing position as a writer and reduces the total open interest in that series on its option exchange.

CLOSING SALE TRANSACTION   A transaction in which an investor who is the holder of an outstanding option intends to liquidate his position by "selling" in a closing sale transaction an option of the same series as the option previously purchased. This cancels the investor's pre-existing position as a holder and reduces the open interest in that series.

COMMODITY FUTURES   Contracts for the future purchase or sale of any of several agricultural or mineral products traded on an organized exchange.

COMMON STOCK   A certificate evidencing a share of ownership or equity in an enterprise.

CONTRACT   In options, a contract is an agreement to buy or sell 100 shares of the underlying stock on demand of the option owner.

CONVERTIBLE SECURITY   A preferred stock, debenture or bond which provides for its conversion into the common stock at the option of the owner and under specified conditions.

COVER   To buy securities for delivery against an earlier short sale.

COVERED CALL   A call which has been sold short, but which is protected against a premium increase because the seller owns the underlying stock, a convertible equivalent, or another option as a hedge.

COVERED WRITER   A writer of an option who, as long as he remains obligated as a writer, owns the shares or other securities convertible into the underlying stock covered by the option.

DIVIDEND   The distribution of cash or securities to holders of a company's stock.

EXCHANGE-TRADED OPTION   A call or put which is listed for trading on an option exchange, and therefore may be purchased or sold readily at any time securities markets are open.

EXERCISE PRICE   See STRIKING PRICE.

EXPIRATION MONTH   The month in which the option privilege ends. Information regarding the exact date should be acquired from a broker, also the final date for trading the options, which is a day or two earlier.

FUTURES   A contract giving the buyer the right to buy or sell a specific commodity or stock until a specified date. The term has been used exclusively in reference to commodity trading, but it is now just as appropriate to describe options.

HEDGE   A means of protecting against financial loss by establishing simultaneous long and short positions in similar, but not necessarily identical, securities.

HORIZONTAL SPREAD   See TIME SPREAD.

IN THE MONEY   A call which has intrinsic value because the current market price of the stock is above the striking price of the call.

INTRINSIC VALUE   The dollar difference between the price of underlying stock and an option's striking price when it is in the money.

LIMIT ORDER   An order to buy or sell which can only be executed under certain specified conditions.

LONG   A security position where the investor is a net owner.

MAKER   The writer or seller of an original option contract.

MARGIN ACCOUNT   The agreement an investor makes with a broker to purchase stocks on credit using previously owned stocks or cash as collateral; also used to support option-writing responsibility.

MARKET ORDER   One placed for immediate execution on the best basis the broker can negotiate.

MARKET PRICE   The last sale or best price that can be realized at a specific time. When buying, it may be the offering price, or when selling, the bid price.

MARKETABLE OPTIONS   See EXCHANGE-TRADED OPTIONS.

NAKED CALL   A call option sold short. The seller owns no underlying stock or other options for protection against an advance in the stock's price and the call's premium.

NYSE   The New York Stock Exchange, the "Big Board."

OTC   Over-the-Counter Market. The term refers to any security transaction not conducted on an established exchange. It is handled through negotiation rather than an auction market and is used for every type of security. Prior to CBOE in 1973, all option transactions were only traded OTC.

OTC CALL   A call not traded on a national exchange.

OPEN INTEREST   The number of option contracts remaining open, that is, which have not yet been completed by the sale or repurchase of the options previously sold, or by the actual delivery of underlying stock through exercise of the option.

OPENING PURCHASE TRANSACTION   One in which an investor intends to become the holder of an option.

OPENING SALE TRANSACTION   One in which an investor intends to become the writer of an option.

OPTION   A call or a put or a combination of two or more calls and puts.

OUT OF THE MONEY   A call having no intrinsic value because the current market price of the stock is below the striking price of the call.

PHLX   The Philadelphia Exchange. This is primarily a regional stock exchange and the third exchange to be approved for trading options.

POINT   One point equals one dollar per share. The term generally is used in reference to 100 shares, when it represents $100.

PORTFOLIO   The securities holding of an investor.

PREMIUM   The price at which an option is traded. The term "price" is reserved for reference to the underlying stock.

PRICE   Refers to the market value of underlying stock and the amount (striking price) that must be paid with the call in order to exercise the option privilege.

PRICE/EARNINGS RATIO (P/E)   The result obtained by dividing the current market price of a stock by its earnings per share.

PRICE SPREAD   A hedged option position in which the trader is both long and short the same number of calls, which are identical except for their striking prices.

PROSPECTUS   A circular containing basic data filed with the Securities and Exchange Commission regarding new securities and their issuer. Option exchanges have a common prospectus, which a broker must deliver to each trader when they enter their first transaction.

PSE   Pacific Stock Exchange. A California regional stock exchange, approved for trading options in April 1976.

PUT   The opposite of a call. A stock option contract that obligates the writer (seller) to accept delivery of 100 shares of a named stock at the striking price at any time prior to its expiration. Puts not traded on an option exchange must be contracted OTC.

RATIO SPREAD   A hedged option position where the trader is long and short an unequal number of calls that are identical except for their striking prices.

SANDWICH SPREAD   A hedged option position where the trader is short two or more calls, protected by long calls with striking prices above and below that of the shorts.

SERIES OF OPTIONS   Options of the same class having the same exercise price and expiration time.

SHORT SALE OF A CALL   The original sale of any call. It may be covered by underlying stock, convertible securities or another suitable call. Calls may be repurchased to avoid exercise, but a short call that expires out of the money need not be bought back.

SHORT SALE OF STOCK OR WARRANTS   The sale of stock not presently owned. Every seller must at some future time purchase an identical security to replace that which was borrowed and sold short—even warrants that are about to expire with no intrinsic value.

S.M.A.   Special Miscellaneous Account, used with margin accounts to make available to an investor all the credit permitted by Federal Reserve System regulations. This buying power often is greater than is apparent by considering only the equity value of the account vs its market value.

SPECULATOR   A person who is willing to risk loss of his principal in exchange for an opportunity to obtain large capital gains.

SPREAD   In marketable options, this is a hedged position with two or more nearly identical calls on a single stock bought and sold simultaneously, either at different striking prices or expiration dates.

STOCK CERTIFICATE   A paper that represents legal ownership of a specific share of a corporation's equity.

STRADDLE   A double stock option (one put plus one call) with identical striking prices and expiration times, which entitles the holder to deliver (a put), and/or demand (a call), the underlying stock at the striking price.

STRAP   A combination of stock options consisting of two calls and one put.

STREET NAME   Stock whose title has been assigned to a brokerage firm (presumably on Wall Street) to hold the account of an investor, who then becomes the beneficial owner. All securities in a margin account are carried in street name.

STRIKING PRICE   The agreed-upon price at which stock will be transferred if an exchange-traded option is exercised. The exercise price of an OTC call, however, is the striking price reduced by dividends paid on its underlying stock during the life of the call.

STRIP   A combination of stock options consisting of two puts and one call.

TIME VALUE   The amount of option premium remaining after deducting the call's intrinsic value.

UNCOVERED WRITER   A writer of naked calls. One who does not own the underlying stock or its equivalent security to protect calls he has written.

UNDERLYING STOCK   The common stock which is subject to call by the owner of an exchange-traded option.

VERTICAL SPREAD   See PRICE SPREAD.

WARRANT   A certificate issued by a corporation which permits the owner to buy shares of its common stock at a certain price for a specific time, or perpetually. Warrants resemble calls in many ways, but initially have a much longer life.

WRITER   A person who sells calls, usually on stock that he owns or purchases simultaneously.

Data on Optionable Stocks
As of May 14, 1976

Industry Group	Stock Name	Where Option Trades	Stock Price 5/76	Stock Beta	% Est'd Div'd Yield (next 12 mos.)	Est'd Current P/E Ratio
Aerospace	Boeing	CBOE	33¾	.89	2.9	10.2
	Gen'l Dynamics	CBOE	60	.86	NIL	8.5
	TRW, Inc.	AMEX	33¾	1.34	4.0	9.2
	United Technologies	CBOE	67⅝	.73	3.5	7.3
Agricultural Equipment	Deere & Co.	AMEX	64¾	1.21	2.9	9.4
	Int'l Harvester	CBOE	25½	1.11	6.3	5.9
Air Transport	Braniff Int'l Corp.	PHLX	12⅛	1.99	2.0	9.2
	Delta Air Lines	CBOE	44¼	1.59	1.4	13.9
	Northwest Airlines	CBOE	31⅜	1.66	1.5	10.3
	Tiger Int'l	AMEX	15⅜	1.36	2.7	7.3
	UAL, Inc.	CBOE	25⅞	1.71	2.3	70.3
Aluminum	Alum. Co. of America	CBOE	53⅜	.71	2.5	20.6
Apparel	Levi Strauss & Co.	PSE	46¼	1.20	1.8	6.2
Auto & Truck	Ford Motor	CBOE	57⅝	.75	4.1	5.9
	General Motors	CBOE	69¾	.80	4.9	8.3
Bank	Chase Manhattan	AMEX	28	.88	7.9	6.5
	Citicorp	CBOE	34	1.18	2.7	12.1
	Morgan (J.P.) & Co.	PSE	58⅜	1.03	3.1	11.8
Broadcasting	Am. Broadcasting	PSE	32	1.05	2.6	19.7
	CBS, Inc.	CBOE	52¾	1.18	3.1	11.5

These Beta factors are more recent than those used in the text examples. Furnished courtesy Daily Graphs, P.O. Box 24933, Los Angeles, CA. 90024
Est'd Dividend Yield and P/E Ratios, courtesy Value Line Investment Survey

Industry Group	Stock Name	Where Option Trades	Stock Price 5/76	Stock Beta	% Est'd Div'd Yield (next 12 mos.)	Est'o Curre P/E Rati
Building	Jim Walter Corp.	CBOE	41	1.13	2.8	9.9
	Johns-Manville	CBOE	29⅝	.92	4.7	9.0
Chemicals	Allied Chemical	PHLX	37¼	1.28	5.0	7.5
	American Cyanamid	AMEX	24¾	1.00	6.0	8.1
	Diamond Shamrock	PSE	67½	1.24	3.0	9.1
	Dow Chemical	CBOE	108⅞	1.29	1.8	15.1
	Du Pont	AMEX	151⅝	1.13	3.7	13.5
	GAF Corp.	PHLX	14⅞	1.21	4.0	7.5
	Grace (W. R.)	AMEX	27⅛	1.09	6.3	7.5
	Hercules, Inc.	AMEX	34¼	1.08	2.4	15.
	Int'l Minerals	CBOE	34⅛	.52	6.0	4.
	Minnesota Mining	CBOE	27¼	1.16	2.5	20.
	Monsanto	CBOE	97	1.23	2.8	8.
	Union Carbide	AMEX	72⅞	1.22	3.5	11.
	Williams Companies	CBOE	21¾	.70	4.2	6.
Coal & Uranium	Pittston	PHLX	44	1.28	2.3	8.
	Utah Int'l Inc.	CBOE	56½	.92	2.1	10.
Conglomerates	Gulf+Western Ind.	CBOE	24	1.06	2.5	5.
	Int'l Tel. & Tel.	CBOE	27	1.24	5.8	7.
	Loews Corp.	CBOE	27⅞	1.47	5.0	4.
Distilling	National Distillers	AMEX	24⅞	.77	5.8	7.
Drug	Abbott Laboratories	PHLX	43⅜	1.33	2.0	15.
	American Home Prod.	AMEX	32⅜	1.07	2.9	19.
	American Hospital Sup.	CBOE	36⅞	1.43	.9	21
	Baxter Travenol Labs.	CBOE	37½	1.25	.5	24
	Johnson & Johnson	CBOE	85⅞	.72	1.3	24
	Lilly, Eli	AMEX	50¾	.81	2.3	18
	Merck & Co.	CBOE	73⅝	.95	2.1	22
	Pfizer, Inc.	AMEX	28⅝	1.28	2.9	13
	Rite Aid Corp.	AMEX	16⅝	1.82	1.4	13
	Searle (G. D.)	AMEX	14½	1.23	3.5	9
	Sterling Drug	AMEX	17	.98	4.1	12
	Syntex	CBOE	27⅞	.88	1.7	12
	Upjohn Co.	CBOE	40⅝	.59	2.6	15
	Warner-Lambert	AMEX	33¾	1.48	3.0	14
Electrical Equipment	Avnet, Inc.	AMEX	17	1.79	3.3	6
	General Electric	CBOE	51	1.23	3.4	14
	Raytheon Co.	CBOE	52¾	1.31	2.1	1C
	RCA Corp.	PSE, CBOE	26½	1.24	3.6	14
	Teledyne, Inc.	PHLX	56¾	2.15	NIL	6
	Westinghouse Elect.	AMEX	15¼	1.11	6.5	6

Industry Group	Stock Name	Where Option Trades	Stock Price 5/76	Stock Beta	% Est'd Div'd Yield (next 12 mos.)	Est'd Current P/E Ratio
Electric Utility	American Elect. Pr.	CBOE	21⅝	.70	9.1	8.4
	Commonwealth Edison	CBOE	27⅜	.73	8.7	8.4
	Consolidated Edison	AMEX	16⅞	.87	9.4	4.3
	Southern Co.	CBOE	14⅝	.68	9.5	8.2
	Va. Electric & Power	PHLX	13¼	.72	9.5	7.3
Electronics	AMP. Inc.	CBOE	33½	1.38	1.3	32.4
	Motorola, Inc.	AMEX	54¼	1.30	1.3	22.6
	Nat'l Semiconductor	CBOE	45¼	2.10	NIL	30.7
	Texas Instruments	CBOE	121⅞	1.15	.8	31.1
	Zenith Radio	AMEX	32¾	1.26	2.9	15.9
Finance	Household Finance	AMEX	17	1.52	6.1	6.6
Food Processing	Beatrice Foods	AMEX	24⅜	1.14	3.7	12.3
	General Foods	CBOE	29	1.07	5.2	9.3
	Norton Simon, Inc.	AMEX	19¼	1.80	2.9	9.3
Household Products	Clorox Co.	PHLX, PSE	11⅞	1.68	4.3	9.8
	Colgate-Palmolive	CBOE	25¼	1.28	3.1	14.0
	Procter & Gamble	AMEX	88⅜	.85	2.5	17.6
Insurance	Aetna Life & Cas.	AMEX	25½	1.31	4.2	8.5
	INA Corp.	CBOE	36¾	.86	5.7	11.6
	Transamerica	PHLX	11	1.25	5.8	8.1
Investment Co.	ASA Ltd.	AMEX	23	.26	4.3	NMF
Machinery	Black & Decker	CBOE	24⅝	1.26	1.8	21.8
	Caterpillar Tractor	AMEX	88¾	1.26	2.5	12.5
	Fluor Corp.	CBOE	35½	1.37	1.7	10.1
Metals & Mining	Asarco, Inc.	AMEX	17	.81	3.5	17.0
	Engelhard Min. & Chem.	PBW	33¼	1.27	3.0	8.0
	Homestake Min.	CBOE	38⅜	.25	3.3	17.7
	Kennecott Copper	CBOE	34⅝	.51	1.4	24.1
	Phelps Dodge	AMEX	43¾	.74	4.9	17.0
	Texasgulf, Inc.	CBOE	35⅜	1.12	3.6	9.5
Mobile Homes	Fleetwood Enterprises	AMEX	18⅛	1.37	1.9	20.5
	Skyline Corp.	CBOE	18¾	1.02	1.3	27.5
Natural Gas	El Paso Co.	AMEX	14⅜	.82	8.2	5.5
	Tenneco, Inc.	AMEX	27⅝	.86	6.5	6.3
Office Equipment	Burroughs Corp.	AMEX	99¾	1.30	.7	23.6
	Control Data	CBOE	22⅝	1.96	NIL	8.9
	Digital Equipment	AMEX	163⅞	1.18	NIL	26.4
	Honeywell, Inc.	CBOE	45	1.75	3.2	10.7

Industry Group	Stock Name	Where Option Trades	Stock Price 5/76	Stock Beta	% Est'd Div'd Yield (next 12 mos.)	Est'd Current Ratio P/E
	Int'l Bus. Mach.	CBOE	252¼	1.08	3.1	17.0
	NCR	PSE, CBOE	28½	1.40	2.5	10.7
	Sperry Rand	CBOE	48	1.41	1.7	11.5
	Xerox Corp.	CBOE	49⅞	1.31	2.2	12.9
Oil Field	Halliburton Co.	CBOE	52⅜	.96	1.0	12.3
Services	Santa Fe International	PSE	29⅝	1.36	1.3	10.0
	Schlumberger Ltd.	CBOE	78	.84	1.0	18.5
Paper & Forest	Boise Cascade Corp.	PHLX	27⅞	1.72	2.9	9.9
Products	Crown Zellerback	PSE	44⅜	1.16	4.3	10.0
	International Paper	CBOE	74⅞	1.06	2.9	12.0
	Louisiana Pacific	AMEX	14¾	1.47	1.7	10.6
	Scott Paper	PHLX	21⅝	1.49	3.5	9.6
	Weyerhaeuser Co.	CBOE	47⅞	.96	1.7	22.2
Personal Ser.	McDonald's Corp.	CBOE	57¾	2.32	.2	23.3
	Sambo's Restaurants	PSE	16⅛	1.94	1.3	9.1
Petroleum	Amerada-Hess Corp.	PHLX	21¾	.72	1.6	5.4
	Atlantic Richfield	CBOE	95⅜	.56	2.7	12.0
	Cont'l Oil	PHLX	69½	.86	2.8	8.0
	Exxon Corp.	CBOE	97⅛	.87	5.7	8.5
	Gulf Oil	AMEX	25⅛	.71	6.5	6.6
	Kerr-McGee Corp.	CBOE	68⅞	.91	1.9	13.4
	Louisiana Land Exp.	PHLX	25⅞	1.12	4.3	11.6
	Mesa Petroleum	AMEX	25⅞	1.10	.4	15.5
	Mobil Oil Corp.	CBOE	57¾	.91	5.8	6.9
	Occidental Petroleum	CBOE	15¾	1.06	6.3	10.5
	Pennzoil Co.	CBOE	30⅜	1.40	4.3	8.9
	Phillips Petroleum	AMEX	54¾	1.28	3.2	10.0
	Standard Oil (Cal.)	AMEX	36¼	.88	6.1	7.4
	Standard Oil (Ind.)	CBOE	47⅜	.61	4.8	8.2
	Sun Oil	PHLX	33	.55	4.5	5.7
	Tesoro Petroleum	CBOE	15½	.87	6.3	5.3
	Texaco, Inc.	AMEX	26⅞	.82	7.4	7.9
	Union Oil (Cal.)	PSE	47¾	.73	4.4	7.0
Precision	Eastman Kodak	CBOE	101¼	1.13	2.2	23.7
Instrument	Hewlett-Packard	CBOE	106	1.33	.3	31.7
	Polaroid Corp.	CBOE	34¼	1.62	.9	15.
Publishing	Simplicity Pattern	AMEX	15¾	1.36	3.1	14.
Railroads	Burlington Northern, Inc.	CBOE	42⅝	.91	2.9	5.7
R.E.I.T.	Fed. Nat'l Mortgage	CBOE	14⅛	.95	6.1	7.

Industry Group	Stock Name	Where Option Trades	Stock Price 5/76	Stock Beta	% Est'd Div'd Yield (next 12 mos.)	Est'd Current P/E Ratio
Recreation	AMF, Inc.	AMEX	20	1.39	5.9	10.5
	Brunswick Corp.	CBOE	16	1.61	2.8	8.4
	Disney (Walt) Prod.	PSE, AMEX	54	2.07	.3	22.9
Retail Stores	Kresge (S. S.)	CBOE	35⅞	1.19	.9	19.1
	Penney, J. C.	AMEX	52	1.32	2.4	15.2
	Sears Roebuck	CBOE	68	1.10	2.8	16.0
	Tandy Corp.	AMEX	38⅜	2.15	NIL	11.0
	Woolworth (F. W.)	PHLX	23	.93	5.2	7.8
Savings & Loan	First Charter Fin.	AMEX	13⅞	.96	NIL	7.0
	Great Western Fin.	CBOE	17	1.07	2.8	7.3
Security Broker	Merrill Lynch & Co.	PSE, AMEX	26⅛	1.66	3.1	7.8
Soft Drink	Coca-Cola	CBOE	81½	1.59	3.2	18.3
	Dr. Pepper	AMEX	14⅝	1.78	2.8	18.5
	PepsiCo., Inc.	CBOE	74¾	1.61	2.7	15.8
Steel	Bethlehem Steel	CBOE	42	.93	5.2	9.7
	U.S. Steel	AMEX	83	.84	4.1	9.4
Telecommuni- cations	American Tel. & Tel.	CBOE	56⅝	.59	6.6	10.1
	Comm. Satellite Corp.	PHLX	27½	.83	3.6	5.8
	Cont'l Telephone	AMEX	13¼	.91	7.3	9.4
	Gen. Tel. & Elect.	AMEX	26⅛	.77	7.2	7.8
	Western Union	PHLX	17⅞	1.11	7.8	9.3
Tire & Rubber	Firestone Tire	PHLX	22⅝	.88	4.8	8.5
	Goodyear Tire	AMEX	21¼	.97	5.5	8.2
Tobacco	Philip Morris	AMEX	55⅜	.99	1.9	13.8
	Reynolds Industries	CBOE	59⅛	.73	5.2	7.6
Toiletries	Avon Products	CBOE	44	1.35	4.0	17.2
	Gillette	AMEX	30	1.25	5.0	10.5
	Int'l Flavors & Frag.	CBOE	23¾	1.10	1.3	29.4
Travel Services	Holiday Inns, Inc.	CBOE	13½	1.72	2.9	11.2
	Howard Johnson Co.	PHLX	13	1.86	1.8	10.6
	Marriott Corp.	PHLX	15⅞	1.64	NIL	18.5
Truck & Bus	Greyhound Corp.	AMEX	16¼	.51	6.1	7.7

Suggestions for Option Record Keeping

Option traders do not find ordinary stock record forms satisfactory because puts and calls involve such a variety of transactions and tax results.* The four basic put and call, long and short transactions, plus limitless hedge combinations, require much more comprehensive records than the comparatively simple data needed for stock ownership. Then too, option trading can create varieties of U.S. income tax liability. Unfortunately, most option traders merely accumulate transaction confirmations, then once a year attempt to sort them out and segregate them by tax classification. Such a non-system is costly because it imposes an irksome annual burden on the trader, but, even worse, it may lead to extremely wasteful oversights and errors throughout the year.

Of course, you could have a system consisting of a dozen different option forms. One might be used to record long calls, others for short calls, long puts, short puts, spreads, straddles, short-term gains, short-term losses, long-term gains, long-term losses, positive income and negative income.

The great advantage of the following system is its simplicity. Here you have a single form and procedure for recording all option information as it happens. It automatically gives all the data you will need to complete your income tax return on options the following year. Most important, it will also contain all the facts to monitor and close your open options safely and systematically during the year.

One reason it is so easy to use this system is that you always start by recording your opening transaction from the left-hand side of the page, whether you bought or sold a call or a put, covered or naked. Then "option watching" helps you monitor open positions. Closing

---

* Sherwood B. Gaylord is the author of the recently published *J. K. Lasser's Stock Option Record Book.*

transaction data are recorded (whether a sale or purchase). You can immediately record the net gain or loss under the proper tax classification for your return next year, and check the tax status of your gains and losses at any time during the current year.

```
┌──────────────────────────────────────┐
│                                        │
│        opening transaction             │
│                                        │
└──────────────────────────────────────┘
```

· *Action*—Suggest you use abbreviations, such as B for bought, W for wrote, S for sold, SN for sold naked, etc. Enter C or P in column headed "Call or Put."

· *Quantity*—The number of options in the transaction. Remember that each option represents 100 shares of the common stock.

· *Corporation Symbol*—The ticker symbol of the common stock.

· *Call or Put*—Use C or P.

· *Expires*—An abbreviation for the month is adequate. (The Option Expiration Calendar on page 190 would be filled in with exact dates.)

· *Exchange*—CBOE, AMEX, PHLX, PSE, etc.

· *Opening Date*—Will show on your broker's confirmation.

· *Gross Premium*—Use dollars and fraction per share. Example: 4½.

· *Net Premium*—The net amount paid or received after commissions, as shown on your broker's confirmation.

· *Stock Price*—This is not needed for tax purposes, but it can be useful to record the approximate stock price on the day you opened the option transaction.

· *Stock Cost*—This information is necessary only when you have written a call covered by owned stock. Should the stock be called away from you, your tax gain or loss will be based on the difference between the original cost of the stock and the exercise price plus the premium of the call. It will be long term if the stock has been owned more than six months.

```
┌──────────────────────────────────┐
│                                    │
│        option watching             │
│                                    │
└──────────────────────────────────┘
```

· *Option Symbol*—This may be used in checking intra-day prices.

· *Long or Short*—Use L or S. A reminder for timely closing.

· *Plan to Close* @—At what premium will this reach your goal?
· *Stop Loss* @—If you guessed wrong, where do you want out?
· *Initial Margin*—How much cash or S.M.A. (Special Miscellaneous Account) is required?

```
closing
```

· *Date*—When the option was terminated or closed out.
· *Closing Premium*—Gross dollars and fraction per share.
· *Net Dollars*—Dollars paid or received after commissions.
· *Gain or (Loss)*—The difference between your opening and closing transactions.
· *Tax Line Number*—Which tax situation applies?

Option Expiration Calendar

If you own options your judgment will become centered around the answer to one question: When should they be closed or exercised? In-the-money options often lose their time value several weeks before the termination date. Of course, when the day and hour of expiration pass, all value is lost—they become absolutely worthless. You must not let this happen to your options.

Suppose, however, that you have short options. Those who have purchased them are in control of the situation, until you buy them back in a closing transaction. Remember that options which are far in the money are likely to be called from you or put to you at any time with no advance warning.

Which of your shorts are most likely to be exercised? Any with some or all of these characteristics is probably vulnerable: one far in the money, trading with little or no time value, about to go ex dividend—especially if the dividend is large or there is a big extra cash dividend. Under these conditions you should either close out your shorts or be prepared to pay a round-trip commission on the underlying stock—assuming you do not already own it.

Of course, it is not absolutely necessary that you purchase the stock immediately when your short calls are exercised. You can stay short the stock, if you have sufficient cash or S.M.A. (Special Miscellaneous Account) in your margin account. However, most option writers not

Put and Call Option

Line	Action	Quantity	Corporation Symbol	Call or Put	Expires	Exchange	Opening Date	Gross Prem.	Net Premium	Stock Price	Stock Cost	Striking Price	Option Symbol	Long or Short	Plan to Close @	Stop Loss @	Initial Margin
							opening transaction							option watching			
1	SC	5	ITT	C	Jan.	CB OE	7/24	1 15/16	$909	18	$—	20	ITT AD	S 1/16	—		$—
2	SN	5	SKY	C	F	CB OE	9/26	2 1/4	1063	15 1/2	—	15	SKY BC	S 1/16	2 1/2		—
3	B	2	BRY	C	Ju	AMX	7/15	1 5/8	351	23	—	25	BRY AE	L 4	7/8		—
4	BP																
5	SP																
6																	
7																	
8																	
9																	
10																	
11																	

covered by owned stock plan to buy back any in-the-money options before they are forced to pay two substantial commissions on the stock transaction.

The Option Expiration Calendar has been designed primarily to help avoid large losses that you would surely incur if you should overlook the expiration dates of any in-the-money options, whether you are in a long or short position. However, this record also can be useful in other ways. For example, it warns you that options are nearing the end of their lives, so you may close them out before the last day or week. It

Buy (Long) and Sell (Short) Transactions

	closing				income tax records					
					year 19_____					
					1	2	3	4	5	6
					Income		Short-term		Long-term	
Date	Closing Prem.	Net Dollars	Gain or (Loss)	Tax Line Number	+	—	Gain	Loss	Gain	Loss
1/6	1/16	$37	$872	1	$ 872	$	$	$	$	$
1/6	2 3/8	1251	(188)	2		188				
1/13	1/4	25	(326)	4				326		

also shows your option commitments scheduled for each month and can alert you to any major unbalance among various option expiration periods.

The Calendar starts by making reference to the page and line numbers on the preceding option form, where complete data on the transaction are given. In this way the Calendar need only summarize your overall position and identify how you originally planned to close each option which expires that particular month.

Names of months would not be printed on this page, so that you

Your Option Expiration Calendar 1976

Page	Line	Quantity	Symbol	Long (L) or Short (S)	Expect to: Buy, Sell, Hold or Exercise	When?
				January		
1	1	5	ITTAD	S	Hold & Buy	Jan.
1	3	2	BRYAE	L	Sell	Jan.
2	1	1	HAL	L	Sell	Jan.
				February		
1	2	5	SKY BC	S	Cover @	2½
2	2	5	FIR	L	Sell	Jan.

can write them in where needed. This allows you to use the form most efficiently, allowing only the space you require each month. This Calendar should, of course, be considered as an integral part of the "option watching" section in the preceding option-record form.

Variations in Call Premiums Vis-à-Vis Underlying Stock Prices

Options—The Shadows of a Stock

Options relate to underlying stock as shadows to the object that casts them. That is why you must always keep your eye on the stock's price movement. Your option decisions will be most successful when they are based on thoughtful anticipation of the stock's probable move and the amount of time you allow for it to happen.

Whether your stock market activity is influenced by earnings and other fundamentals, by technical analysis involving study of historic stock-price patterns, or by no formal system, you also need to understand the different ways that the premiums of a stock's various options are likely to be affected by changes in the stock price.

You can start to gain this kind of experience by studying the several stock and related option graphs in this section. Each set includes brief comments to aid you in recognizing typical premium patterns with changes in stock price.

The larger stock graph charts the daily high, low and closing prices. Each smaller option graph shows similar information for the call premium (right-hand scale). The thin wavy continuous line (left-hand scale) is the daily closing price of the stock.

There is also a slightly heavier horizontal line connecting the call's striking price on the left with the "0" call premium point on the right. If the stock price is below this line the call has no intrinsic value—only time value. When the stock price is above this base line, the call does have intrinsic value, plus time value. These graphs show January calls which expired the previous day and therefore traded at about their intrinsic value; or, if they were slightly out of the money and traded at all, at the minimum price of 1/16.

191

An upper set of vertical bars at the bottom of each graph indicates the volume of options traded each day in units of 100 shares each. The lower set of vertical lines is the call's premium expressed as a percentage of the common stock's closing price.

For in-the-money calls this percentage represents only the time value portion. Intrinsic value has been deducted for reasons explained in Chapter 13. The premium percentage for out-of-the-money calls is equal to the negative intrinsic value plus actual premium, divided by the current stock price. In either situation the graph's percentage represents the gross profit which could be realized if calls were written against owned stock and later exercised by the purchaser. You can convert this into an approximate annual rate of return by dividing "Trade Days Left" into 250 and then multiplying this by the indicated premium taken from an up-to-date chart.

· Note that both the January 45 and 50 calls were in the money at midyear (1975) when Telephone stock was over 50. By September only the 45's were even slightly in the money. During this three-month period the January 45 call fell from a high of around 9 to about 1⅜, while the January 50 dropped from a 5⅜ high to ½. This illustrates that when the stock price declines sharply, the lower striking-price call loses more dollars, but the one at a higher striking price falls by a greater percentage.

· Telephone's stock began a steady 4-point advance in October and the January 45 call moved with it point for point. Notice, however, that the January 50 remained virtually flat during this time, the premium ranging only ½ point above and below 1. Note, too, the "Premium" percentage on the charts, which shows both options lost time value rapidly, even though the stock price continued to rise after the calls were definitely in the money.

· Observe the great increase in volume of January 50 calls sold during January when the stock rose from 50 to 54 and the option premium and intrinsic value ranged between 0 and 4. With time value at zero much of that period, purchase of a January 50 call at $100 to $400 offered 10 to 20 times more leverage and far less dollar risk than the simple conservative purchase of 100 shares of Telephone common stock at $51 to $54.

· The patterns for the midi- and long-term calls, April and July 50's, were quite similar, beginning in late October, when the Julys first traded. Their only real difference was a premium spread, about ⅜ points more time value in the longer call. It is important to remember that Telephone pays a substantial quarterly dividend (at that time 85 cents, but currently, of course, 95¢ per share). This was reflected in the lower

American Telephone and Telegraph

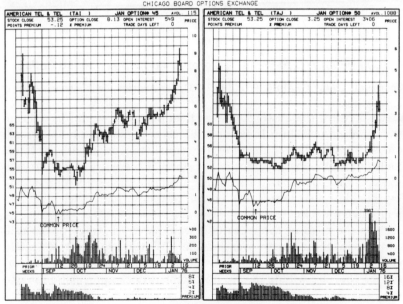

Figure 16

American Telephone & Telegraph: January 45 vs January 50 Calls

Courtesy of DAILY GRAPHS, P.O. Box 24933, Los Angeles, Calif. 90024

American Telephone and Telegraph

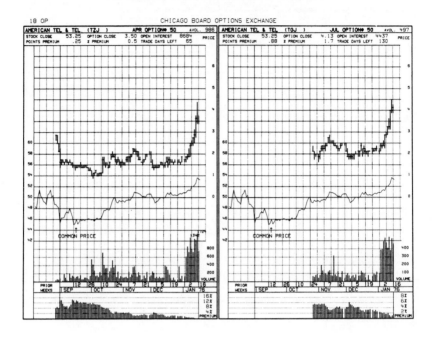

Figure 17

American Telephone & Telegraph: April 50 vs July 50 Calls

Courtesy of DAILY GRAPHS, P.O. Box 24933, Los Angeles, Calif. 90024

spread between these two premiums than otherwise would have been considered normal. In this example, 85 cents (⅞ point) plus ⅝ spread equals 1½ points. This is almost exactly equal to 1% per month for three months times the market price of the stock. It thereby fits the formula developed in Chapter 12 for a normal minimum time-spread premium. You should be alert to similar premium relationships in other high-div-idend-paying stocks.

On the basis of these charts it would seem that Telephone call premiums favor the buyers over the sellers. Writers apparently are moti-vated to sell Telephone calls to provide insurance more than income or growth. They are willing to give up potential stock appreciation in ex-

Texaco

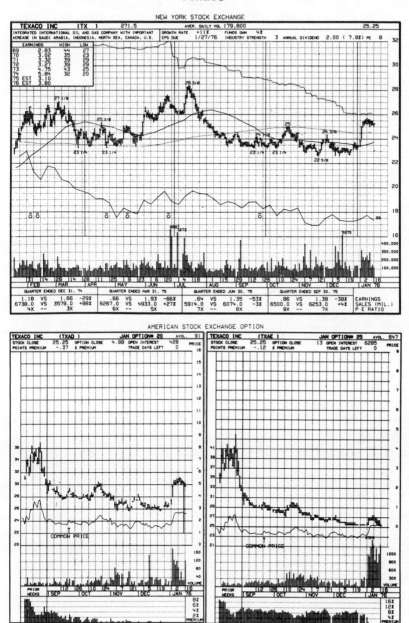

Figure 18

Courtesy of DAILY GRAPHS, P.O. Box 24933, Los Angeles, Calif. 90024

change for the protection offered by the option's intrinsic value, plus a relatively low time value and the substantial Telephone dividend.

· The TX January 20 and 25 calls illustrate option premium variations *vs* a stock price that remained nearly flat over most of the calls' lives. This example shows also how a vertical spread, written in September with the 20 call long and the 25 short, would have worked out during this particular price action in TX stock. The January 20 call could have been purchased at about 4 (only ½ point over its intrinsic value) when the stock was at about 23½. The short sale of a January 25 call would have realized about 1, making a 3-point spread. The January 25 call never went in the money until very near the end of its life, although it almost got there about Oct 20. Its premium then bounced back to over 1, but by that time the 20 call had advanced to 5, increasing the spread to nearly 4 points. By the January expiration, spread between call premiums had increased to the 5 points of difference in their intrinsic values; when the stock price advanced to a small fraction over 25, this put both calls in the money.

· Note that the stock price rose about 2¼ points, or 10%, during the first two weeks of January. The January 20 call also increased 2¼ points, but this was a gain of 75%. The January 25 call premium only increased about ½ point, from 1/16 to 9/16, but this represented a substantial move of about 800%.

· The U.S. Steel January 70 call provides two dramatic illustrations of the tremendous variation which followed only moderate changes in the price of underlying stock. Notice that in weeks prior to September the stock price was never above 65, and that the January 70 premium high was 6. Then the call plunged to 1¾ in early September, while the stock price fell only 5%. Late in September the stock climbed to 71¾, and at that point the call shot back up to 6. But then, for the rest of the year, it was all downhill as the premium collapsed virtually to zero in December. This sinking spell continued even when the stock climbed back above 66, higher than in August when the call premium was 6, but of course the remaining option life then was much greater.

· Notice what happened early in January, the last two weeks of this option's life. The stock rose sharply, 9 points, or 15%. However, this caused the January 70 call to advance from 1/16 to nearly 6, a maximum gain of almost 100 times or 10,000%. This is a dramatic example to option buyers of how a relatively little advance in a stock's price can sometimes turn a cheap, about-to-expire "casino call" into a highly profitable speculation—also, to option writers, of how going naked can leave you stripped (explained further in Chapter 20).

U.S. Steel

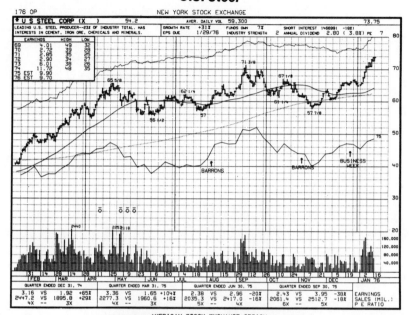

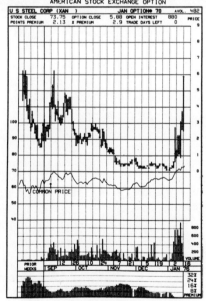

Figure 19.

Courtesy of DAILY GRAPHS, P.O. Box 24933, Los Angeles, Calif. 90024

Index

Airplane, flying analogous to option trading, 168
Aggressive-defensive strategies:
  use of options in sharp decline, 104–107
  via selling calls, 103
  see also Conservative-aggressive strategies; Investment strategies
Amerada Hess, 72
American Stock Exchange (AMEX), 13, 15, 37, 42, 43, 48, 100, 147, 159
American Telephone & Telegraph (AT&T), 73
  buying calls *vs* buying stock, 55–56, 58
  commissions on stock *vs* calls, 60
  price and time flexibility of calls on, 68–70
  stock price movement related to calls, 192, 193 (graph), 194 (graph)
  writing in-the-money calls on, 86
AMEX, *see* American Stock Exchange
Arbitrage, 123, 124
Atlantic Richfield, 72
  hedging with, 124
At-the-money calls, premiums for, 86
AT&T, *see* American Telephone & Telegraph
Automobile insurance:
analogous to equity insurance via calls, 101–02
  collision, analogous to buying calls, 57–58
Automobile rental:
  analogous to option trading, 13, 21, 31, 44
  see also Avis; Hertz
Avis:
  car rental, analogous to buying call, 13
  company size compared to AMEX, 38
Avon Products, 26, 112

Barron's, 36
Baruch, Bernard, attitude toward speculation, 66
Bearish price spreads, 137–41
  Merck chart, 140
  striking price and month for, 141
Bearish-speculative strategies, with naked calls, 50–51
Bear market:
  diversified option program in, 73
  loss of time value in, 79
  of 1971–74, 169
  ratio spread in, 141–42
  reinvesting option income in, 90
  selling naked calls in, 154–55
Beta Factor, 22, 77, 116, 179–83
  and estimating time value, 34
  high, 72
  as measure of stock's volatility, 77
Bethlehem Steel, leverage provided by calls on, 64–65
Broker, role in option trading, 21
Broker's commission, deregulation of, 60
Bullish attitude toward buying calls, 171
Bullish price spread:
  chart, 138
  techniques for using, 136–37
Bull market:
  diversified option program in, 73
  premium time value in, 79
  selling calls in, 86
Burroughs, 72
Butterfly spread, *see* Sandwich spread
Buying calls, 116, 118
  as alternative to buying stock, 46–47, 55–56
  bullish attitude toward, 171
  as conservative-aggressive strategy, 45–47
  flexibility as investment, 67–70
  four reasons for, 13–14